P9-CFQ-028

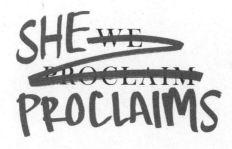

SHE ~~WE~~ ~~PROCLAIM~~ PROCLAIMS

★

Our Declaration of Independence
from a Man's World

JENNIFER PALMIERI

GRAND CENTRAL
PUBLISHING

NEW YORK   BOSTON

Copyright © 2020 by Jennifer Palmieri

Cover design by Elizabeth Connor
Cover copyright © 2020 by Hachette Book Group, Inc.

Hachette Book Group supports the right to free expression and the value of copyright. The purpose of copyright is to encourage writers and artists to produce the creative works that enrich our culture.

The scanning, uploading, and distribution of this book without permission is a theft of the author's intellectual property. If you would like permission to use material from the book (other than for review purposes), please contact permissions@hbgusa.com. Thank you for your support of the author's rights.

Grand Central Publishing
Hachette Book Group
1290 Avenue of the Americas, New York, NY 10104
grandcentralpublishing.com
twitter.com/grandcentralpub

First Edition: June 2020

Grand Central Publishing is a division of Hachette Book Group, Inc. The Grand Central Publishing name and logo is a trademark of Hachette Book Group, Inc.

The publisher is not responsible for websites (or their content) that are not owned by the publisher.

The Hachette Speakers Bureau provides a wide range of authors for speaking events. To find out more, go to www.hachettespeakersbureau.com or call (866) 376-6591.

Library of Congress Cataloging-in-Publication Data has been applied for.

ISBN: 978-1-5387-5065-0 (hardcover), 978-1-5387-5210-4 (large print), 978-1-5387-5066-7 (ebook)

Printed in the United States of America

LSC-C

10 9 8 7 6 5 4 3 2 1

For Janice Enright and Evelyn Lieberman

You wanna fly, you got to give up the shit that weighs you down

Toni Morrison,
Song of Solomon

★

CONTENTS

PREAMBLE

★

Whereas, in the course of human events, it becomes necessary for people to dissolve a set of beliefs, biases, and behaviors that fail to recognize the inherent value of one half of the population and perpetuate impediments to achieving all that their God-given rights and talents entitle them to;

We proclaim, as women who continue to live in a world in which we are undervalued and underrepresented in positions of power relative to men, our declaration of independence from a man's world.

$\mathcal{I}$n July 1848, four women sat at Mary Ann M'Clintock's kitchen table in upstate New York to draft the Declaration of Sentiments and accompanying resolutions that were to be presented at the Women's Rights Convention at Seneca Falls later that month. Seated alongside M'Clintock was women's rights leader and Seneca Falls organizer Elizabeth Cady Stanton, along with Mary Ann's grown daughters, Elizabeth and Mary Ann.

These women gathered at a time when they had virtually no power in the eyes of the law. Giving women the right to vote was considered so radical an idea that even some of the movement's most ardent supporters argued against including a demand for suffrage in the Seneca Falls resolutions. The women who drafted the Seneca Falls document believed their situation to be dire, and the language of the Declaration of Sentiments reflects both their desperation and their certainty in the cause—arguing that women in America had been "aggrieved, oppressed, and fraudulently deprived of their most sacred rights" as citizens. There was no precedent for their actions; all they had was faith in their own abilities and in the inherent righteousness of their crusade. Stanton brought some draft versions of the document with her to the M'Clintock home for the women to work from, but they were not satisfied with what they had produced until one of them had the idea to model the Declaration of Sentiments on the Declaration of Independence itself.[1]

Seventy-two summers earlier, Thomas Jefferson had committed to paper the radical concept that it was "self-evident, that all men are created equal," so Stanton and the M'Clintock women amended Jefferson's sentence to include two universalizing words: "We hold these truths to be self-evident: that all men and women are created equal." Using the founding fathers' own words and formula to validate women's equality positioned it as a natural progression of the principles upon which America was founded. I admire their ingenuity. Despite their efforts and commitment to their cause, however, another seventy-two years would pass before women finally secured the right to vote, on August 18, 1920. But it was through the perseverance of those women and their successors that the right was eventually secured, and in their honor I chose their declaration as a model for my own.

For the time has come for the women of America to make a new declaration. One hundred years after women won suffrage, we still live in a world where men hold the vast majority of power and women are consistently undervalued relative to them. Despite all women have done to fit in, and all that well-intentioned men have done to help us along the way, we have only been able to rise so far in this man's world. It is no longer serving us well. We should not continue to prop it up by following its rules. It is time to declare our independence and proclaim the start of an exciting new era for women—an era in which we break from a world that does not value us enough and create a place where we are able to reach our full potential. I see millions of women in America waking up to the same realization—this man's world was never our destination. It was never ours. We have always been visitors here, and now we are moving on to create our own space.

I want to be clear that this is not a declaration against men. I do not believe that men are my enemy, nor do I feel my life has been one long exercise in subordination to them. Like many women, I learned a lot observing how men work, had male mentors, and gained some invaluable skills as I attempted to model myself after them. Those skills I acquired served me well and will continue to help all of us going forward. But I believe we have gone as far as we can following a man's model. After decades of making so many strides, we reached a plateau. A man's path turned into our rut. Our dependence on the old male models and our belief that following their path would eventually work out for us has ended up sustaining the very power systems that keep women from succeeding.

In the fall of 2017, I began work on a book called *Dear Madam President: An Open Letter to the Women Who Will Run the World*. Less than a year after my former boss Hillary Clinton lost her historic bid to become the first woman president, writing a letter of advice to the future first woman president and insisting that women *will* run the world could seem to some like a bold move—but not to me. Because at my core I believed in my own ability and in the ability, strength, and sheer willpower of women in America, and so did millions of other women.

Just look at everything women in America have accomplished in the last two years. We turned out by the millions as part of Women's Marches. In both 2017 and 2018, women ran for elected office in historic numbers, and won by historic numbers, too. Today in America, there are more women starting their own businesses than ever before. Women accounted for 40 percent of business owners in 2018.[2] In 2019, America saw not one but *six* women stand on the national debate stage to compete to become the next president of the United States. And starting in the fall of 2017, women who had been sexually assaulted and harassed by men stood up and demanded that they be held accountable as part of the MeToo movement. It was a watershed moment for efforts to even out the power dynamic between men and women in the workplace.

I see the 2017 Women's March as the turning point. It is when I first saw women break away from the world we had known. The march was held the day after President Trump's inaugural and just a couple of months after we had lost the 2016 presidential election.

My normal reaction to losing a political campaign is to leap up and start fighting again as soon as possible. I thought that this was my duty; that if I did not pick up the fight, no one else would. Like a lot of women, I had spent my career with an outsize sense of what was my responsibility. I thought if I did not dive for every ball, no one else would be there to catch it. And if I let any ball drop, I would not be let back into the game.

But the 2016 defeat took more out of me than the average campaign loss. It made me question a lot of the assumptions I had made about my place in the world, including whether my effort mattered at all. I was not ready to just jump back into the fight, not without being sure there would be a point in doing so. Instead, I decided to watch and see what America would do in that moment.

So I stood on the sidelines for the Women's March and watched as millions and millions of women dove for the ball. As soon as I saw the news reports detailing the numbers of women who'd turned out for the march, I knew that women had turned a corner for good. Women in America had each other's backs in a way I had never experienced before, and it made me grateful beyond measure. It also gave me hope.

Much of what women need to proclaim now was on display in the Women's March—the power of women supporting other women, the resolve of women who know they should be valued as much as men, and the ability of one woman to make a difference. Those are the tenets we need to embrace now.

Suffrage gave women tools to pry open entrance to the man's world. Women finally had political power and could advocate for themselves, and they began to infiltrate the many industries that had been reserved only for men for so long. For many years, it had felt like we were making consistent progress—and then the momentum sputtered out. We plateaued, found ourselves banging up against the same glass ceilings. A 2018 study done by the Center for American Progress presented a compelling portrait of all the ways women's progress has stalled in the workplace.[3] The report noted that after decades of women making economic gains, the narrowing of the gender wage gap decelerated in the 1990s and 2000s and the percentage of women in management jobs stalled. Women accounted for only 5 percent of all CEOs in the 2018 Fortune 500. Consider this one telling fact alone: There were more CEOs named James in the Fortune 500 in 2018 than there were women CEOs. More than a hundred years after the first woman was elected to Congress, men still hold nearly 75 percent of the seats in Congress, and only nine out of the fifty governors are women.

I remember seeing a story in the *New York Times* detailing how there were fewer female CEOs in

America in 2018 than there were in 2017.[4] I didn't find the downturn in female representation surprising or even demoralizing. It was validating. It was confirmation of what I already knew. Women aren't doing it wrong; there's just nowhere else for us to go in this world that was built for men. It can no longer contain us.

An exciting number of women have already broken out. They are the women who marched, who ran for office, who broke out on their own to start a new business, who refused to be intimidated by men who had abused them. These women are the ones who cannot be defeated, who know they deserve more, who don't listen to the rules in the man's world that say they do not have power, do not have options, cannot succeed, or have to behave according to the old rules for women. They know better. It is time to follow the lead of these women who are well on their way to running the world. It is time to finish the job they started—they and the millions of women who fought for women's equality before us—by declaring our independence from this man's world.

In the two years since I wrote *Dear Madam President*, I have sought to learn more about the women who fought for suffrage. I am no historian and by no means an expert, but I have immersed myself enough to feel like I know some of these women. They were human, and that means they were flawed. There were different factions within the suffrage movement, and they were often at odds with each other. But these women were also pioneers. They could not look to history to learn from the experiences of others who'd worked to advance women's rights, as we have the benefit of being able to do.

The story of the M'Clintock women happens to resonate with me. There are more such stories I will share in the hope that they will inspire you to learn more about the fight for suffrage and to see your own struggle reflected in these women's stories. We are part of a long line of women who have been pushing for equality, and I hope that knowing their stories will make you feel, as I do, that we owe them our own commitment to the cause.

The Declaration of Sentiments enumerates the many ways women were treated unfairly in nineteenth-century America. Most of their grievances—the inability to vote, or to own property, or to earn wages independent of their husbands—were injustices that had been enshrined in law. The ways women were held back were easy to identify and, even though not all who attended the Seneca Falls Convention supported suffrage, in the end they affirmed the belief that giving women political power through the right to vote was the best solution for addressing women's problems.[5] And they were right. However, it took too long to win suffrage and to address all of the inequities laid out in the Declaration of Sentiments, because those efforts took place squarely within the man's world. By declaring our independence from that world, we are free to effect the changes we seek immediately, in real time.

The obstacles that are holding women back now are less easy to identify, as are the best ways to tackle them. Without question, America should ratify the Equal Rights Amendment; having women's rights enshrined in the Constitution is long overdue and would provide women with important protections. But the truth is that there's no silver bullet law that would change the anti-equality biases that continue to exist in the minds of both men and women.

Which is why I have written this book: so we can explore the beliefs, biases, and behaviors that exist in the world—and in our own heads—

that hold women back, and then declare our independence from them. We will take new stock of the knowledge, skills, and strength that we have developed during our time in the man's world that make us better prepared to succeed now. Declaring our independence from the man's world means we are going to stop being dependent on it for our success, and stop expecting it to work out for us the way it has for men. Instead we will proclaim the undeniable power that has been in women all along, pushing us to this point. We will harness the power we have to change the world.

Just as the women in Seneca Falls had to make the declaration that it was self-evident that men and women were created equal, we must proclaim our own freedom and our worth. Let the world know that women will no longer be dependent on broken models not built for us. And so, like the M'Clintock women, I sit at a kitchen table to write a new declaration—this one written at a home in Missoula, Montana, the birthplace of the first woman ever elected to the US Congress, Jeannette Rankin. She was elected in 1918, two years before the suffrage amendment was ratified, and has the distinction of being the only woman to have voted in Congress to give women the right to vote. She could have been born anywhere, but she was born in Missoula. I write here drawing inspiration from her spirit and all the good ghosts of the women who came before us who saw how their world needed to change and believed in their own power to bring it about.

Chapter Two

MAN'S WORLD, I'M JUST NOT THAT INTO YOU

★

Whereas, the long trail of obstacles women have faced in a man's world has evinced its design as one created by men, for men;

We proclaim that it is our right, it is our duty, to throw off the fetters that have hindered our progress and to provide new guards for our future security and fulfillment.

$\mathcal{I}$f you are a woman in the workplace today, you have been trying to succeed in a world that was designed for someone else. The foundations of the power systems under which business and government operate today were established hundreds of years ago by men, and they were specifically designed to accommodate men. I was going to say they were designed to exclude women, but I doubt those men believed women would ever be capable of rising up far enough to bother excluding them. Women were simply ignored in their plans, and that deeply embedded thinking continues to exist today. I do not say this to suggest we are defeated or to make us victims, but to acknowledge this history, to accept that the man's world can never be our final destination, and to proclaim that we are throwing off the constraints that have held us back and moving on to someplace better. Considering all the obstacles women have been pushing up against for all of human history, it is amazing what we have been able to do here.

Women are told to fight the imposter syndrome—that pesky feeling that we don't really belong in the positions we hold. But there's a kernel of truth behind the imposter syndrome: We are attempting to succeed in a workplace that was built by men, for men. Of course it doesn't feel natural to us, and of course men fit into it better. It was designed for them. We need to reorient our thinking and behavior accordingly, and toward that end let us imagine what it would be like for men if women had been in charge from the start.

Consider how men would feel if women had created all the power systems we live under, all the forms of government, currencies, economic systems. Think about how America might be different if at the time of our founding 250 years ago, it had been women who decided how our government would be run, and they had decided that only women should vote.

Imagine how men would feel about their place in the world if for their whole childhood their families spent a good part of Saturdays and Sundays watching women play sports on TV. Every Friday night, the boys would see the whole town turn out to watch the high school girls play soccer as they watched from the stands or cheered the girls on from the sidelines. And imagine that boys also played sports, but their games were squeezed in either early or late in the day, making sure that the prime spots were held for the girls' teams.

How might men feel about their own voices if every speech they heard from an American president growing up was delivered by a woman and most of the songs on the radio were by women? Try to imagine how different our perspective would be on what stories and art we found important and inspiring if the people who decreed what "good" art was and decided whose stories got published, what movies and television shows got made, had always been women instead of men. Or what men might internalize about their personalities if all but one of the late-night television show anchors—the people we hold up as the prototype for what an engaging, charming, trustworthy host looks like—were women? Might it make them worry about their own personalities and whether they were likable enough?

Finally, consider how men would feel about their chances at succeeding in business, science, the arts, media, or government if they saw that the vast majority of leaders in all those fields were women. It is doubtful men would go bounding into the workplace, brimming with confidence, blissfully assured of their rightful place there.

Feeling uncertain of themselves, they would look for subtle clues about how they were expected to behave. It is likely they would feel uncomfortable speaking up in a meeting in which they were the only man, surrounded by nine women. They might try to mimic women's leadership styles. They would have no other model to follow, after all. They might read and write a lot of books about how to succeed in a world that was not made for them. Try to convince each other to support one another and not fight other men for what they imagined was a limited number of seats available for men at the table. And imagine that all along we, as a society, had thrown at them a bunch of conflicting signals about what we valued in men and how they were supposed to behave differently than women—but at the same time, men saw that the people with the real power were the women.

Sounds like a tough place for men, doesn't it? And yet women have managed to find a way to thrive while laboring in exactly these difficult circumstances. It makes me proud to be a woman. It should make us all proud.

Intellectually, I understand how it came to be that men were the ones who created all the power systems. History is full of those lessons. But despite that history, I have never believed that women were meant to live in a world where they are subordinate to men. Rather, I have always believed that my own abilities and those of all women are equal to men's. Fortunately, there have always been women in the world who knew they were equal to men and pushed to improve women's standing.

The foundations of the business and political systems that exist in the world today trace back to two historical transitions from the seventeenth and eighteenth century—the rise of capitalism and industrialization, and the creation of democratic systems that acknowledged individual rights. This history is relevant to us and our quest today. The systems put into place at that time continue to impede women today. It is also considered to be the beginning of the modern women's rights movement.

In *No Turning Back: The History of Feminism and the Future of Women*, women's studies scholar Estelle Freedman describes a "revolution which transformed women's lives" as having occurred over the last two centuries.[6] She pinpoints the revolution as having started at the time of the two aforementioned historical transitions. Prior to the creation of capitalism and the age of industrialization, women and men were entwined in more of an economic partnership—going all the way back to the times of hunters and gatherers. Men hunted; women gathered. And while, as they have for all of human history, men exercised dominance over women, some semblance of a balance of power existed between the husband and wife under this arrangement and on through to agrarian times. Men and women were reliant upon each other for survival. As Freedman describes, capitalism disrupted the sense of "reciprocal relations" between husband and wife. The rise of industrialization and capitalism—which freed men in many ways from the confinement of old feudal and other power systems—had the opposite impact on women, making them more economically dependent on men. Likewise, while America's Declaration of Independence was considered a radically progressive document in its time by claiming the rights of the individual, it also specifically delineated that those rights belonged only to men.

Still, even during those times, there were women who knew they deserved better and began advocating for women's rights. In 1792, the British writer Mary Wollstonecraft wrote what is considered the first articulation of women's inherent rights, *A Vindication of the Rights of Woman*. It followed an anti-monarchy piece fueled by the French

Revolution she had written called *A Vindication of the Rights of Men* in which she argued that kings did not have divine rights over men. In *A Vindication of the Rights of Woman*, Wollstonecraft applied that same principle in support of women, arguing that just as kings did not have divine rights over men, men did not have divine rights over their wives. She wrote of women's rights, "I do not wish them [women] to have power over men, but over themselves."[7] The two-hundred-year battle for women's rights we still wage today had been joined.

There was a time when I would bristle at the suggestion that I was a woman trying to make it in a man's world. When my female friends in the Obama White House would sometimes lament this, I would tell them I thought it was self-defeating for women to concede that this was a man's world, particularly after we had all worked so hard to fit in to it. In my mind, proclaiming ourselves to be women in a man's world cheapened my own standing in the White House and in the broader workplace. It made me feel like I wasn't in the game and not really a competitor. I felt like it devalued all I had accomplished.

Now I see how wrongheaded that thinking was. What I believe now is that acknowledging we have been women trying to compete and succeed in a man's world does not cheapen what we have accomplished, *it makes what we have accomplished more valuable*. It means our gains were by definition hard-earned and that we were pioneers. Knowing that we've managed to thrive as we have should be a source of great pride and motivating self-confidence going forward. As Ann Richards, the first female governor of Texas, said in her 1988 speech to the Democratic National Convention, paraphrasing a famous quote, "After all, Ginger Rogers did everything Fred Astaire did. She just did it backwards and in high heels." We should value all the exhausting effort we put into the work we do, all the ways we've pushed ourselves to perform better than the men lest there be any question about our abilities, and all the skills we've had to develop to succeed in a man's world. The efforts we made will serve us well going forward.

And now we are proclaiming that we're officially done with this man's world. We have learned what we could, we've proven all we needed to prove, and we are moving on. After spending decades trying to succeed in a man's world, it has lost its allure for us. Man's world, we are just not that into you.

There could be some element of self-preservation

taking hold here. A person can develop disdain for a place where she does not feel valued. But a deeper awakening is happening in women's minds and souls. We are realizing that this man's world is not worthy of our time and effort. Even if the kind of success powerful men achieve was readily available to me, their brand of success is not particularly fulfilling to me. Too often success here is defined only in relation to money and retaining power. It all amounts to zero-sum games. There is too much money and power constricted into too few hands, and it is no longer serving anyone—women or men—well. Women need to be paid what we are worth, and the fact that so many are not remains a grave inequity that must be addressed. But making money is not the only measurement of success. I think success is having the freedom and ability to put your best effort into something that will make a difference in the world. That is not possible when living under the kind of constraints women have faced.

This man's world represents the past. It is built on outdated premises of what should be valued in the world, and it excluded women from the start. It can never be our future. A place that underappreciates us, limits our growth, and makes us doubt our own abilities is never going to be a place where women can thrive. We have to shake off the doubts that have plagued us and look beyond the limited opportunities that have existed for women in the man's world and imagine new possibilities for ourselves. For some of us, that may mean joining the ranks of women who have decided that their place of employment did not offer enough opportunity and started their own business. For others, it may mean pushing to revitalize their current workplace so women have better chances for advancement. For me, it has meant refusing to believe that women over fifty can't start new careers as writers. Declaring our independence from a man's world does not have to require a radical change in the circumstances of our lives. It does require a radical change in our outlook on life, however: namely, that we will no longer accept second best as women's lot in life. We are going to expect and demand better for ourselves. As the women in America today, we proclaim, with pride for all we have accomplished and confidence in all we have to offer, that we are moving on to build a future in which we are able to realize our full potential.

Chapter Three

INFINITE

★

Whereas, we reject the societally implied notion that there are a limited number of women that can succeed in the world and that the professional advancement of women is a zero-sum game;

We proclaim that the opportunities for women to succeed are infinite.

$\mathcal{I}$ had a comparatively easy time fitting in to a male-dominated workplace, but I saw that it was a lot harder for some women and I always felt an obligation to help them. I felt the need to be discreet about it lest my male colleagues think I had an agenda and was pushing to promote women for the sake of female empowerment without regard to the best interests of the larger enterprise.

I also avoided being noticeably aggressive in advocating for my female colleagues because I worried it could undermine the overall standing of women in the workplace if it seemed like we were constantly requiring special attention. Not only would it make it harder for us to fit in, but it would also play in to any number of false stereotypes about women. I was therefore very careful about picking my battles.

My devotion to the cause was by no means monolithic; there were times when I wondered if the woman I was helping would end up outshining me, perhaps one day even taking my place. But I decided to banish such thoughts because I did not want to be the kind of woman who jealously guarded her own success as if it were part of a zero-sum game in which only a select few women could participate at any one time. I wanted to be a sister, and going forward, I would always try to look upon female newcomers to the workplace not as potential rivals but as percentage points ticking ever upward toward that magical 50 percent mark.

Eventually, I had to change my thinking because like most people, I had been buying in to all the flawed premises that help prop up the man's world: that women have to sneak in while men aren't looking, that we require some special dispensation to be hired or promoted as if we are a charity project, and that we are in direct competition with each other for a limited number of slots—in short, that the professional world belongs to men, and women are only visitors.

We have to fully reject the notion that the professional advancement of women is a zero-sum game or we will make it true, because—like most mistaken beliefs—it is self-perpetuating. Moreover, it is the opposite of reality in that our individual success as women is linked to the success of other women. We are intertwined with other women as part of a larger struggle, and real, sustained progress for each of us is dependent upon other women also being valued and succeeding. It is truly a situation where "all for one and one for all" applies.

There's no question the 2016 election represented an awakening for millions of women in America. I think those of us who worked for Hillary Clinton feel a special obligation to band with other women and support each other now. Our motivation is partly about who she lost to, but it is mainly the experience of watching our brilliant, compassionate, modest candidate being reduced to a caricature by her opponents and even by the press that made us realize that women had to band together from here on in. If that kind of gross public distortion of character could happen to her, it could happen to any woman.

In ways large and small, women are subjected every day to the kind of subtle gender bias and blatant misogyny that Hillary encountered throughout her campaign. The election brought into stark relief for us the fact that this isn't just about electing the first woman president or getting more women on corporate boards, although both of those things would be great. It is about women being respected and valued the same as men, which has to start with believing in ourselves and supporting each other unconditionally. I am no longer worried about whether men think I am trying to help women at the cost of the larger enterprise; for me, helping women *is* the larger enterprise.

The women's rights movements in this country have ebbed and flowed in strength over the last two-hundred-plus years. The first wave of the suffrage movement led by Susan B. Anthony and Elizabeth Cady Stanton saw the effort stall with Congress's failure to pass a suffrage measure in 1879. In Winifred Conkling's book *Votes for Women*, she describes the biggest enemy of suffrage at the end of the nineteenth century as being indifference rather than opposition. The movement entered a doldrums phase

Elizabeth Cady Stanton predicted that the generation of women following her would not exhibit the "infinite patience we have for half a century," and she was right.[8] Her own daughter Harriot Stanton Blatch, along with Alice Paul and Lucy Burns—all of whom spent time as part of the more radical British suffragette movement—would become tireless organizers of women for suffrage in the early part of the twentieth century. They would sometimes clash with the older groups and with women like Carrie Chapman Catt of the established National American Woman Suffrage Association, which favored more moderate tactics;

rivalries even formed within the movement. But ultimately the women were aligned in their shared goal, and the movement was revitalized. There does not seem to have been a single precipitating event that pushed the young women of Blatch's generation to pursue suffrage with more urgency, just a certainty that it was an idea whose time had come.

I believe we are in a similar moment now. The women's rights movement has been in a holding pattern for the last few decades. I will admit to some complacency myself in that I definitely wanted to help women get a foothold into the workplace, but I also thought we were on the right track and was settling for a slower pace of change than I should have. It turns out that track was a rut. We were being allowed a steady diet of small victories to keep us placated. But now decades of the doldrums are giving way to a renewed sense of urgency and the opportunity for new and more politically aware generations of women to band together for the purpose of achieving true gender equality.

Millennial women in America today feel the most dissatisfaction with the state of women's standing relative to men. Like the young suffragist leaders from the early twentieth century, the women entering the workplace a hundred years later are no longer content with women's second-class standing. This group is the most likely of all demographics to believe that men in America have it easier than women. As part of a 2017 study done by the Pew Research Center on attitudes about gender equality in the United States, respondents were asked whether men or women had it easier in America today.[9] The overall result for all ages was that 36 percent of respondents said that men had it easier, 9 percent said women had it easier, and 56 percent said there was no difference. When millennial women were asked this question, 52 percent of them said men had it easier than women, 3 percent said women had it easier, and 45 percent saw no difference between how the two genders were treated. Comparatively, only 37 percent of GenX and Baby Boomer women said they found men had it easier in the country today.

This particular GenXer is with the millennials. In certain key areas, such as salary and workplace upward mobility, men still have dramatic advantages over women, and if we continue the trend, parity will remain tantalizingly out of reach for a long time. Each year, the World Economic Forum produces a Global Gender Gap Report, which calculates the year at which women can expect to achieve gender parity with men. Among the metrics it measures when determining the gap is the relative standing of women to men in income, leadership positions in government and business, and the state of their health. The most recent report, produced in December 2018, determined that based on current rates of change it will take more than two hundred years before gender parity is achieved.[10] The number is so astonishing it would be comical were it not so outrageous and unacceptable. We are not waiting two hundred more years for common sense to be allowed to prevail.

There is good reason why millennial women especially are feeling the limitations of the man's world. After decades of making gains in the workplace, progress has slowed by some important measures that affect millennial women and those of the younger GenZ generation. A 2019 McKinsey study on women in the workplace done in partnership with LeanIn.org showed that even with more educational opportunities available to women than ever before, they are still facing stubbornly resistant plateaus in the workplace.[11]

Women have outnumbered men on college campuses since 1988,[12] and for many years they have earned more bachelor's degrees. Nevertheless, the McKinsey study clearly showed a phenomenon referred to as the broken rung: Men got 52 percent of the entry-level jobs, compared with 48 percent for women, despite women earning more bachelor's degrees. It also found that women were less likely than men to get promoted to manager level: For every hundred men who are hired and then promoted to manager level, only seventy-two women make it. Additionally, men hold 62 percent of manager-level positions in corporations. Some might argue that this is proof the system is working. Well, yes, it is working, but since women constitute 50 percent of the population, it is obviously working better for men; until half the managers and half the CEOs and half the corporate board members out there are women, and until the salary gap disappears, it is merely evidence that the system is working exactly as it was designed—by men, for men.

In 1977, the sociologist Rosabeth Moss Kanter developed the 30 percent tipping theory, which applied the critical-mass theory to women in the workplace.[13] Kanter's research led her to conclude that women needed to make up at least 30 percent of a workplace before they were in a position to operate at their full potential. This is what it takes to normalize women in leadership positions, so they are not seen as an "other," but are appreciated for whatever skills they bring to the job, just as any man would be. Below 30 percent, they tend to be dismissed as tokens by their male colleagues and not considered equal.

Once women hold 30 percent of the membership of a board, or leadership of an organization, they are in a position to truly change the institution and also to advocate more for other women. When women are at less than 30 percent, they can feel uneasy about advocating for other women colleagues. There is a lot of pressure to assimilate when you are in the minority; you want to be seen as valuable to the organization and you certainly don't want to stand out as a gender equality activist. At the 30 percent mark and above, when women leaders advocate for more women to join the institution, they are perceived as making acceptable personnel decisions rather than as fighting to swell the ranks of women as part of an agenda. Getting to the 30 percent tipping point for women in positions of leadership needs to be our goal. After that, we will be able to contribute our best work, and more qualified women will be brought into the fold. Indeed, another study done by LinkedIn for the World Economic Forum's Global Gender Gap Report found that when women are better represented in leadership roles in companies, more women get hired.[14] The report found that having senior women in leadership was a top indicator for hiring women at all levels, thus helping develop a pipeline of women for more leadership roles. Female success is a renewable resource, not finite. More women in the room begets more women in the room. And what I know is that any room gets better with more women in it.

Too often having women or other underrepresented people at the table is presented as some kind of gift bestowed on them by the men in power. The suggestion is of a one-way street where the person granted admission is the only one with something to gain in the arrangement. It neglects to take into account all that the person has to contribute. John Podesta, a former boss and long-time mentor of mine, has always made it a priority to hire women and people of color. He told me that he does not do this just to give someone an opportunity, although that is important. He does it because having a diverse workplace—whether in the White House or on a campaign or at the think tank he created—made the work better. Having more perspectives represented around the table and contributing ideas produces better results.

In the last few years I have taken on new projects, from writing a book to working on a new podcast and projects for television. It has meant working with new groups of people, and every time I walk into a meeting for one of these projects, I look around the room and ask myself, *Where is she? Where is the woman who is going to help make it all work?* Fortunately for me, she has always been there. Often there is more than one of her there. She is the one who has not only great ideas but the emotional intelligence, determination, and stamina needed to get it all done. She makes the room better. It's a small example of a much larger phenomenon I see happening as women grow in strength, and it's making the world better.

At the 2018 Women's March in my home-town of Annapolis, one of the women speakers described a legend that imagines humanity as a bird with a masculine wing and feminine wing. For most of human history, the masculine wing is stronger than the feminine wing. The bird manages to fly despite this imbalance, but eventually the masculine wing becomes overdeveloped, and the bird can only fly in circles. When we get to the twenty-first century, the feminine wing finds a way to harness her power and grow in strength. The new powerful wing frees the bird from its circular purgatory, and it soars to new heights.

No more holding patterns. No more buying in to tropes that only a few of us can succeed at a time. We proclaim that when women band together to support each other, we can contribute to our fullest capacity. Freed from the restrictions of an imbalanced society, the opportunities for us are infinite.

Chapter Four

SISTERHOOD

★

Whereas, we know that all women are our sisters and that when we unite to support each other women succeed, and when we are divided we perpetuate our own second-class status;

We proclaim that we will support other women.

In recent years my women colleagues and friends and I have banded together to support each other in ways I had never experienced before, and we do it with a sense of urgency. I am part of an ongoing text chain with dozens of women, most of whom I have never met in person but who are always available to offer advice, moral support, validation, or a helping hand if anyone in the chain needs it. Until things are truly equal, it's going to be hard out here, and we need to be able to lean on each other. I think we all have the same sense that we are part of an important moment for women in American history and feel an enormous responsibility not to screw this up. The stakes are very high. It feels perilous because although we are on the cusp of finally being able to realize the infinite potential we know we have in us, we are also faced with a patriarchal backlash that threatens to set us back by decades. I feel a sense of agency and an obligation to other women I have never felt before, as well as a reciprocal unity that convinces me we will prevail.

As I wrote in *Dear Madam President*, I did not join the Clinton campaign because I had a life-long ambition to elect the first woman president. I simply believed that Hillary was the best person

for the job. But there were many women supporting the Clinton campaign for whom electing the
first woman president *was* the dream. These are
the women who had been working in the trenches
for decades in support of women's equality. They
had slogged their way through the most recent
set of doldrums the women's rights movement
experienced after the failed ERA battle of the
1970s and early '80s. They were pushing for equality when feminism was no longer in vogue and
women like me wondered why these old-school
feminists continued to make such a fuss. I mistak-
enly believed that women had already successfully
infiltrated the man's world, and that we could lay
down our arms and adapt to the system we were
now a part of.

But these women knew better and kept pushing.
They despaired at the lack of real progress women
were making in the world. As some of them have
explained to me, electing the first woman president took on an added importance in their minds
because having a woman reach the pinnacle of
power in the world would have been confirmation
that, despite their concerns, all the gains they had
seen women make in the previous fifty years were
not slipping away. When Hillary ended up losing

the race, the despair these women felt far eclipsed my own. I saw the defeat as losing round one in this era's bout against the patriarchy. They feared it meant all was lost.

While I managed to find a way to view our loss as the beginning and not the end of this larger battle, I was still pretty shocked to find myself fighting a reinvigorated patriarchy that had so recently seemed to be on its way out. Those of us who had believed it could be completely banished were kidding ourselves, however: Misogyny, racism, and hate are never completely extinguished in the world—at best, they can be marginalized. Keeping them out of the mainstream requires constant vigilance, but fortunately, you also cannot extinguish the determination of women who believe in themselves and each other. The trenches are jam-packed with us now, and because we do appreciate the stakes involved, we will not allow factionalism to divide us.

It is daunting to consider the totality of challenges women are still encountering, some so insidious as to be almost undetectable. But I also feel a measure of relief to finally have it all out in the open and to not have to kid myself anymore that I am doing great in a man's world.

Granted, there is a lot of hate being directed toward women and women's causes these days. It's very upsetting and no one should have to endure it, but it does not discourage me. That hate is just the last stand of the supporters of the patriarchal status quo in their losing battle against the tide of history. Nevertheless, I still felt a gut punch each time a woman dropped out of the presidential race, because I know that the rules of the man's world contributed to her demise. It might have been the higher standard she was held to than her male counterparts, or the intensity of the media scrutiny that is reserved for female candidates, or the corrosive questions about her "electability" that undermined her candidacy just by being asked—most likely, it was a combination of all of these factors and many others in a similar vein. It sickens me because I also know that close to half the voters who have been conditioned to look askance at any female political candidates are women themselves.

The history of the women's rights movement shows that when women don't back each other, women lose. In fact, women's progress has suffered some of its biggest setbacks during periods of division between women. As woman suffrage groups were gaining power in the late 1860s, a counter-effort of women opposed to suffrage started to form. They were referred to as the antis, and part of their argument was that women should not have access to the ballot because they were "influenced by pity, passion, and prejudice rather than judgment." One thousand women signed a petition in opposition, which helped stymie the efforts to amend the Constitution to guarantee women the right to vote. One thousand signatures may not seem like a lot now, but at a time when the US population was considerably smaller it was significant that women had organized to oppose suffrage for themselves. Female voices of opposition had an outsize impact and helped blunt the momentum of the movement.[15]

The antis also argued that suffrage could harm women by taking away the special protections they enjoyed as wives and mothers. The same sentiment would echo in the specious arguments of those who opposed ratification of the ERA by claiming that it would result in widows losing their husbands' Social Security, forcing women to work outside the home.[16] It just so happens that the leaders of both the anti-suffrage movement and the anti-ERA movement were wealthy white women who lived lives of relative comfort and who had nothing to gain by criticizing the patriarchy and biting the hand that fed them. Even now there are women who are convinced there are legitimate reasons for opposing the ERA, but rather than argue with them I just want to remind them that there was a time when women thought there were legitimate reasons for opposing universal suffrage.

Madeleine Albright says there is a special place in hell for women who don't support other women. We are at another inflection point in history when women can either achieve the solidarity necessary to make true gender equality a reality or stay divided and allow a backlash to undo some of our most critical gains, potentially delaying equality for another generation. Therefore, what each of us does in this moment matters. We can all do something to support another woman and help her break through what is holding her back. And if we have a platform, we should use it to advocate for our sisters. There are many women in the world today who work in the arts, business, and sports who are doing just that. I find a couple of stories of professional female athletes particularly inspiring because the women are taking heat for their activism but not letting it faze them—they understand that women have a higher obligation to each other in this moment.

Muffet McGraw is the longtime basketball coach of the Notre Dame women's basketball team. Since 2012, McGraw has had an all-female coaching staff. In the spring of 2019, she gave an interview in which she lamented the rise of men's coaches in women's college basketball and said that she had no plans to hire a male coach on her staff again.[17] She used to have men on her staff and had even made a point of hiring men because she thought it was a positive thing that men took an interest in women's sports, and she felt it added balance to the team. But then she noticed that women coaches were starting to get crowded out of women's basketball. In 1977, nearly 80 percent of college women's basketball teams were coached by women, yet somehow that number was down to 60 percent in 2019, probably as a result of women's basketball finally becoming profitable enough for the man's world to take notice. Meanwhile, the number of women coaching men's college sports remains below 3.5 percent, the same number it was in 1972. McGraw has concluded it is incumbent upon her to give women coaches opportunity. In a press conference where she was asked about her comments regarding not hiring men, she pointed to the failure of the ERA as an example of how women still struggle. "We don't have enough female role models, we don't have enough visible women leaders, we don't have enough women in power."[18] I admire her for using her position to help lift up other women. She saw that women were losing ground on her watch and she is doing something about it.

The US Women's National Soccer Team, which keeps winning World Cup titles, has pushed the fight for equal pay into the spotlight by calling out the gap that exists between their compensation and that of the US men's team, which earns more but has never gotten close to a title. As team co-captain, Alex Morgan described the team's fight for equal pay during the 2019 World Cup: "I had this dream of being a professional soccer player, and I never knew it entailed being a role model, being an inspiration, standing up for things I believe in, standing up for gender equality. But now I don't know a world where I just play soccer. It goes hand in hand."[19] This is the attitude we should all have, and Alex Morgan is the kind of role model we need to see in far greater numbers.

I am writing this book to deliver the message to all women that you are not alone in feeling limited by the rules of a man's world, and that you are part of an awakening sisterhood that will support you in breaking free of those rules in order to realize your dreams. We all need to speak out when we see women being treated unfairly or held to a different standard than their male counterparts. For example, women reporters are often singled out for criticism simply because the aggression that we expect from male reporters is perceived as inappropriate or overbearing in a female reporter. We need to publicly push back against such criticism; treating it like a valid viewpoint just perpetuates the underlying stereotype. Another example is the way women bosses are frequently described as being "difficult" to work for. Well, let's face it, a woman in a traditionally male-dominated corporate leadership role didn't get there by being a wallflower—she had to be tough and driven enough to make it as far as she did, and that toughness and drive can play into the stereotype of the difficult female boss. We must defend our women bosses from the charge of being difficult and start conditioning our culture not to default to these bias-driven mischaracterizations.

If anything, with the pressure women bosses are always feeling to measure up to the man's world double standard, they are to be commended for the level equanimity they do show. We must lessen that pressure by advancing more women to leadership roles in all industries so that more people, male and female, become so acclimated to working for women that it is no longer cause for comment or scrutiny.

When my husband and I lived in Missoula, Montana, over the summer, I had the pleasure of getting to know some of the women working in politics in Jeannette Rankin's home state. Carol Williams has done much to follow in Rankin's footsteps. She is one of the women who never left the trenches and kept fighting all through the doldrums. Carol spent more than a decade in the Montana State Legislature, rising to become the first female Senate minority leader in Montana history. When she entered the legislature, she was frustrated by the lack of growth in the number of women elected to the body. She co-founded a group to help raise money and encourage women to run for office in Montana, and it has been an enormous success. Carol's List, as the group is now called, helped elect so many Democratic women that, for the first time, the 2019 Montana State Legislature hit the magic 30 percent mark of seats held by women. Expect positive change to ensue.

Still, Carol is frustrated that there has yet to be a women president. However, her daughter, Whitney Williams, is now running to be Montana's first female governor. Whitney thinks it is her duty because she understands what is at stake for the country now; the Williams women are certainly doing their part. Carol told me that she had the honor of meeting Jeannette Rankin once. It was at a Washington, DC, dinner party held in the 1970s in honor of Jeannette's ninetieth birthday. Carol used the opportunity to express dismay to Jeannette that women were still battling for equality. She told me that Jeannette laughed and said to her, "My dear, we do not do this work because it is easy, we do it because it is right!"

A millennial friend of mine asked me what I thought the role of her generation of women was in this ongoing struggle for women's equality. I told her that her role was to not expect to be treated worse than the men and to not tolerate it when it happened. That is what all of us must proclaim. It is our obligation to each other as well as to the women who have been in the trenches fighting for hundreds of years to get us to this moment. All of that work, effort, and sacrifice can finally secure what women have always been entitled to but were always denied—the ability to live up to our full potential. It is an honor to be a part of this sisterhood. I know that this time we will not let each other down.

Chapter Five

NICE GESTURES

★

Whereas, we know that being satisfied with the incremental allowance of small gains for women helps perpetuate power systems that have stifled women throughout history;

We proclaim that we will no longer be placated by token gestures that do not lead to substantive progress toward equality for women.

On a cold January day in 1917, President Woodrow Wilson directed a White House usher to venture outside the White House gates and invite a group of suffragettes picketing the president to come inside and enjoy some warm coffee or tea. It was a seemingly nice gesture for Wilson to make given that the women were there to protest his lack of action in support of suffrage. The suffrage leaders were known to him because they had been to the White House many times for meetings to advocate for their cause during Wilson's first four years in office. But this time, the women indignantly refused to come into the White House. They would not leave their posts.

The women outside the White House that day were the Silent Sentinels, a group of suffragist protestors organized by Alice Paul and Harriot Stanton Blatch, daughter of Elizabeth Cady Stanton. Four years prior, on the day before President Wilson was to be inaugurated in 1913, these and other women had organized a historic, and chaotic, march in Washington in support of suffrage. The thousands of women who had turned out for the march were subjected to appalling verbal and physical harassment from hundreds of male spectators. The failure of local law enforcement to adequately respond and protect the women marchers was such a serious matter that the US Senate held two weeks of hearings to look into the matter; the police chief involved was later censured.

But the march succeeded in getting the new president's attention. Two weeks later, Paul and a group of suffragists met with Wilson to seek his support for suffrage. Wilson responded evasively that he had not considered the issue and had no opinion on it. Throughout Wilson's first term, women leaders would come to the White House seeking his support, to no avail. Paul grew so frustrated that she and her organization, the Congressional Union for Woman Suffrage, decided to oppose Wilson's reelection. At the same time, the more moderate National American Woman Suffrage Association (NAWSA) headed by Carrie Chapman Catt continued to work within the political system and eventually got Wilson to declare his support for suffrage at a NAWSA convention in October 1916; it was a month before Wilson's reelection, and he wanted the support of suffragists for his campaign. And while he assured the NAWSA women that they would soon triumph in their bid for suffrage, he did not promise action.

It was Harriot Stanton Blatch who came up with the idea for the 1917 Silent Sentinel picketing campaign after Wilson's reelection. The president had refused to give his blessing to their cause, so the time for meetings was over. The women would stand, silently, in front of the White House to protest the lack of action. The dual symbolism of the act was powerful: When it came to power, women were on the outside looking in, and their political voices had been muted. One year later, in January 1918, President Wilson gave a speech to Congress expressing his support for suffrage.[20]

From the window of my tiny office on the first floor of the West Wing, I could see the spot outside the White House where the Silent Sentinels once kept their watch. The office was small but in a coveted spot just a few yards from the Oval Office. I never would have had the chance to sit in it if these women had not fought for equality from outside those gates.

I am someone who has sought to make change from inside. I know that change requires agitation from both inside and outside power systems. That kind of inside-out strategy is an element of nearly all successful social change movements, including the suffrage movement. But growing up,

I had never been one to challenge power systems; rather I wanted to be *part* of them. I absorbed all the signals that told us men were the powerful and interesting ones and responded not with anger, but with resolve. I pledged to myself that I would simply do what I needed to do to fit into their world.

My first job in the professional world was working in the office of Congressman Leon Panetta in the late 1980s. Leon Panetta was my congressman. I had gone to high school in his district in California, and my parents still lived there. I started interning for Leon in 1986 when I was nineteen, and I worked for him for a full decade. It was a good ten years for us both. He went from being a highly effective congressman to President Bill Clinton's White House budget director and then White House chief of staff. Happily for me, he took me with him in each of those jobs.

I learned a lot about politics from Leon, but what's relevant for this book is what I learned by watching the women I worked with in that first job on Capitol Hill. In retrospect, I realize that I learned lessons about politics from watching both my female and male colleagues, but I mimicked the behavior of the women I worked with. They were the ones to whom I looked to figure out who I should *be* in the workplace. I had seen enough of life to know that I was likely to have a harder path to success than the men did, so I intuited that I had better follow the lead of the women who had managed to get themselves this far.

Those women did not let any ball drop, ever. They were thorough, dependable, and resourceful. They saw around the corner, identified problems ahead of time, and took it upon themselves to make sure those problems got solved. They did not get out over their skis. They always had their facts straight. They did not wing it. They might laugh along with the amusing men we worked with for a few minutes, but sooner rather than later they hurried back to their desks and started working. They were the ones who made everything work.

Another thing I observed in that first position was that the men in our office thought there were boundaries to their jobs. They would weigh in on legislative policy and political strategy and then they would go home for the day, confident that this level of effort on their part was enough. The women in our office did not observe such boundaries. We were always available, and we did not leave until the work that needed to get done, whether it was technically ours or not, got done.

In my own career, I never felt like a man tried to hold me back. Nevertheless, for nearly thirty years I worked harder than most of my male colleagues and often achieved less. There is not a single deliberate act of sexism I could point to that would account for this fact. On the contrary, the men I worked with were supportive of me, they mentored me, they looked out for me, and they gave me opportunities. And they did better than me. They rose faster—I saw it happening. Worse, I expected it to happen. I thought that as a woman making my way through the remnants of the man's world, I would still encounter obstacles along the way. I expected not to advance as fast as the men, and I tolerated it when they jumped ahead of me. Like a lot of women, I ended up working for men who were years younger than me. I eventually got the "big jobs," like becoming communications director for President Obama. But I was ten years older than the man I replaced.

As women, we are often not great at advocating for ourselves. It means we can miss out on raises and promotions we deserve. Looking back on my own career, for example, I see that a combination of fear and pride prevented me from being the good advocate for myself I should have been. I was scared that my requests for more money or a better title would be rebuffed, and then I would have to face the fact that my hard work was not as valued as I thought. I also let pride get in the way. I knew I worked hard, harder than most of the men. I wanted my contributions to be recognized without me having to ask for it. But they never were recognized in that manner. So, like a lot of women, I settled for tokens.

I received a lot of appreciation from my colleagues and bosses. They would laud my dedication and reliability. They would tell me how they could not possibly do it all without me. Their approbation was sincere and was important to me. It proved to me I was valued, but I see now that it was both self-defeating and selfish of me to be satisfied with it. By not pushing for more money or a better title, I wasn't just hurting myself but also contributing to the gender pay gap. I should have been fighting for more money, not just to get paid what I was worth but also because other women's standing was riding on it. If we as individual women allow ourselves to be satisfied with small gains, we might feel a slight economic benefit—but the net gain to working women everywhere is zero, particularly the women who are just making their way into the workforce. We have to fight these fights now so the next generation inherits a world where women not only are paid what they are worth but fully expect to be paid the same as men.

There was one time in my career when I felt like I might actually be getting paid more than I was worth. It was when I was the national press secretary at the Democratic National Committee (DNC) in 2001. Minyon Moore, whom I served with in the Clinton White House when she was the political director, was the executive director of the DNC at the time and is the one who hired me. When she told me how much I would be making, my first reaction was to tell her it was too much. It was not a huge number, but it was still more than I had ever made before.

Minyon could be forgiven if she'd laughed at me, but instead she grew stern. "Jennifer, this is what the other members of the team at your level, men and women both, are making. It is a little more than a government salary would be, but much less than you would make in the private sector. It is what you are worth." She went on to say how important it was that women be paid what they are worth because failing to do so doesn't just hurt you but impacts how other women get treated. None of this happens in a vacuum; women belong to one big sisterhood and what affects one, affects us all. It was good advice and a good lesson but not one I would take to heart as soon as I should have.

The Clinton campaign was part of a transitory phase for me. I started the job in 2015 feeling as if I was in the same world I had inhabited in the Obama White House the year before. But little by little it started to change. Working for the first time in an enterprise that was geared toward lifting up a woman, I felt the ground start to shift under me. There were cracks in the universe that gave me a glimpse of someplace different. I started to see how the world reacted to Hillary differently, and it made me reconsider how I looked at myself and my experiences in the man's world.

Advice from other women helped the process. Early on in the campaign, I went out to dinner with the MNSBC news anchor Mika Brzezinski. I was complaining about how expensive it was to live in Brooklyn, where the campaign was head-quartered, particularly on low campaign salaries, when she interrupted me to say, "I can tell you right now that you are not getting paid what you are worth." I was a little taken aback; I hadn't told her what I was making or how it compared with the salaries of others on the campaign. I cannot recall word for word all she told me that night, but one phrase remains very clear in my mind: "It is written all over your face."

She said she could tell that I was the one who would make it all work, the one who would never drop a ball. I was the one who would not complain about what I got paid, and I was just glad to be there. She had taken all that I believed had made me valuable and special in the workplace, all that I had intuited about how to succeed in the man's world, and turned it on its head. It made me see that I wasn't doing as great as I thought in the man's world; I was getting played. The fact that her one comment had such a big impact on me is telling—it's as if I had been subconsciously waiting to hear it. Some part of me had known all along that I was letting myself be taken advantage of, and I just hadn't wanted to face it.

The next day I went to work, demanded more money, and got it. I became the highest-paid person on the Clinton campaign. It didn't make me feel great—in fact, it felt a little sour. Why did I have to push to get this? Naively, I had wanted the recognition to be bestowed upon me and not to have to quibble for it. It made me consider the other ways I may have let myself be taken advantage of. It was the beginning of my reevaluation of how I had learned to behave according to the rules prescribed by a man's world.

In my life, losing the 2016 election pushed me further along this path of reconsidering my place in the world. For you, it may be a different realization that makes you see you have settled for too little for too long and that doing so hurts not only you but other women as well. The 2016 campaign broke nearly every rule I had ever been taught about how politics worked in America. After losing that race, I was forced to look plainly, without sentimentality, at the men I had worked with and for, at my actual standing, and to face some tough realities. Being the one who made it all work was not helping me; it was helping the man's world run smoothly. I came to realize that I had not been pushing through the remnants of what was left of a man's world, I'd been sustaining it—working hard to uphold a system that perpetuated men's success at the expense of my own and other women's. I decided then and there that unless we take it upon ourselves to disrupt the power systems in a man's world, those systems are self-reinforcing. Generation after generation, they seem to produce more men leading more men.

So now we are disrupting the power systems by proclaiming that we will not be satisfied by small gains for ourselves or other women. We have to learn to walk the balance between being inspired by the gains we fight so hard to achieve and being placated by them. Yes, it's often true that progress happens in small doses, but you have to continually fight for small gains in order to secure the big ones. For example, I was thrilled by the historic wins women enjoyed in the 2018 congressional elections. The women who put themselves on the line and ran in 2018 inspire me a great deal and give me enormous hope for the future—but at the same time, having women hold a mere 25 percent of the seats in Congress is not satisfactory. The old me would have been content with that number, whereas the new me is already looking ahead to 50 percent congressional representation. True equality is reached when parity is reached, and that means women should hold 50 percent of the seats in Congress—that is when we will be satisfied.

In 2018, Stacey Abrams ran a historic race to become governor of Georgia. Had she been sworn into office, Abrams would have been not only the first black woman to become governor of Georgia but also the first black woman to serve as governor of any state in America. On November 16, 2018, after ten days of contesting the results of the election due to the closeness of the race and voting irregularities that were believed to have suppressed the African American vote, Abrams held a press conference to say that she was ending her bid for governor. But she refused to concede, because she found that in many ways the election had been rigged against her through illegal voter purges and other tactics that made it difficult for supporters in poor and diverse communities to vote. As she expected, Abrams was criticized by some for refusing to concede, but it made me admire her all the more. She wrote in her book *Lead from the Outside*, "As outsiders, we are expected to continue on as the system commands, primarily to preserve our ability to participate and just maybe, one day, win the lottery or opportunity to be the one who slips inside the door."[21] Although this sentiment refers to racial injustice, it could just as easily be applied to gender inequality or any other unequal relationship between oppressor and oppressed. The power dynamics are the same.

We proclaim that we will no longer be doing what we are expected to do, or what the old power systems command us to do. We are stepping outside them to push for the big gains that bring women true equality, not small gestures. We are not in the fight just for ourselves but for every future generation of women, and we are never leaving our posts.

Chapter Six

SOUVENIRS

★

Whereas, to achieve the higher standard of performance we have had to meet relative to our male colleagues, women have often worked harder than men and adapted our behavior to be accepted in a man's world;

We proclaim that we will embrace those skills we have developed that serve us well and make us effective and shed the behaviors that we determine to be self-defeating for women.

$\mathcal{B}$etween kindergarten and high school, I went to nine different schools. Moving around that much forced me to develop some valuable adaptive skills that helped me in the man's world, which, for women, is all about fitting in—being feminine in appearance but not in behavior. But just fitting in meant I wasn't becoming the best version of myself I could be. Not that all men are sure of their place in the world, but they don't have to deal with gender bias as they try to work their way up, which leaves them free to concentrate solely on their jobs; as a woman in the workplace, I was always hyper-aware of what I needed to do to fit in, which diverted my focus from other priorities more deserving of my attention. We are consumed with having to read all the signals that tell us how we should behave in order to be accepted into the man's world, and with having to work harder than our male colleagues to prove we belong.

But we should take some time to consider all we do to fit in the man's world, to examine what skills we have developed in the process as well as what things we do that are self-defeating. We should then keep as souvenirs of our experience the best pieces of ourselves and the hardest lessons learned and incorporate them into the women we are now, leaving the rest behind.

As visitors trying to fit in to the man's world, we have had to learn to be very observant. Understanding that women were often not listened to or ignored in meetings, we became very good at reading a room and understanding the power dynamics at the table so we could find the right moment to make our point and have it count. Because we were always looking for ways to make ourselves useful and prove our worth, we made an effort to understand all the elements of any operation we worked in, not just the pieces for which we were responsible. It made us ready to dive in and do whatever was needed to make the place run, and we were happy to do it. We made it our business to understand the people we worked with, too— what motivated them, what they worried about, what they needed from us, and what they needed to hear to feel good about themselves. In this way, we developed our emotional intelligence, and it made us better at our jobs.

My Clinton White House positions exposed me to some of the best political strategists in the world, and I tried to make the most of the opportunity. I did, indeed, learn a lot about strategy, but looking back I think one of the most important lessons I learned was the practical limitations of strategy. What really mattered was what you were able to get done, and that's what I and other women in the White House did— we got things done, sometimes by sheer force of will. We would often quote Shirley Chisholm, the former congresswoman from New York and the first black woman to run for president, who said, "If they don't give you a seat at the table, bring a folding chair." And so we would show up at meetings we had not been invited to, demanding a place. We would tell the guys that if they actually wanted something to come of all the great ideas they were going to discuss in the meeting, they had better have one of us in there. We were the ones who would actually convert their ideas into reality. It worked, and we were let in.

Evelyn Lieberman set the example for the rest of the women in the Clinton White House when it came to commanding respect and demanding to be let into the room. Evelyn started in the White House in a junior job as personal assistant to the First Lady's chief of staff. But she was so effective in actually getting things done and de-livering on results that she rocketed up the ranks from personal assistant to deputy press secretary to eventually holding one of the most senior positions in the White House, deputy chief of staff. She told all the women she mentored, "People take their cue from you." What she meant was that if you believe you have an important job to do, or that you have something to say that matters, act like it and people will respect you. In other words, fake it until you make it.

I eventually worked my way up to White House communications director, but I never let go of the compulsion to be the one who made it all work by putting in the necessary time and effort. Just coming up with ideas isn't getting the job done. It doesn't change anything in the world, and I want to make a difference. My girlfriends in the Obama White House would admonish me for my work style. "A guy wouldn't stay as late as you," they'd say. "I know that," I would reply. "I don't want to do the job the way he would. I want to do it my way."

A number of the women I worked with as relatively junior staff in the Clinton White House held senior jobs in Hillary Clinton's campaign—they include Huma Abedin, Emily Bromberg, Adrienne Elrod, Sara Latham, and Minyon Moore. While we held more senior positions this time around, we had not lost our get-it-done ethos. We were the ones devising strategy, but we also made sure the strategy we devised was something that could and did get implemented. With other women like the formidable Brynne Craig, we formed a cross-departmental unit called Team GSD—Team Get Shit Done. We were in politics to make things happen, to make a difference—not to be show-boats. We held on to the lessons we learned from men that worked for us, like getting things done, and we discarded the old habits and thinking that had held us back, like just wanting to fit in and doubting ourselves.

After our loss in the Clinton campaign, I was surprised to find that some of my colleagues who seemed the most affected by the defeat were men. We were all devastated, to be sure, and the out-come of that campaign changed my outlook on life in very dramatic ways that continue to this day. But there were some men who seemed beaten down by the defeat far more than the women. For me, it was not the first time I saw something I really cared about and put a lot of effort into get caught up and destroyed by larger forces. That had happened to me dozens of times in my life, albeit with far less dramatic consequences. But experiencing this kind of setback was not new to me or to other women. We knew what it was like to feel both disappointed and powerless to do anything about it, and that resilience, which is another quality we bring to the workplace, helped us survive the bitter defeat that no one saw coming.

Women generally set higher standards for themselves at work than men do, not because we are morally superior beings but because we are made to feel the need to work harder and longer just to deserve a seat at that table. *However*, sometimes women can let their drive for perfection get in the way: Always expecting perfection can be crippling when perfection isn't possible, which is often the case. We should let go of the sense that we have to be better than the men. We don't. It's fine if we choose to be, but it shouldn't be a bias-driven compulsion.

I found that the men I worked with in the White House were not surprised to be there. It was part of their plan for their career, and they were pleased but not shocked when their dream was actually realized. It's not that they saw themselves as entitled to their professional good fortune, but it did seem like they expected the pieces to fall into place the way they did—another luxury most working women have been denied. And yet in both the Clinton and Obama administrations, the women generally lasted longer than the men. We stayed the whole time; we didn't have a majority of the most senior White House jobs at the beginning of the term, but we did by the end. I think we worked so hard to fit in and figure out how to do these jobs, we were loath to leave them. We finally felt like we had a solid berth. Given our uncertain status over the years, women tend to like rules and structure in the workplace: They ground us and give us a clear path to follow in a man's world. For this reason, we can be more averse to professional risk than men, though ironically, the real risk for us has become playing it safe. If we want the same opportunities that men have, we have to position ourselves to take advantage of them, and this sometimes means leaving the comfort of security for the unknown.

As for the things I wish to leave behind from my professional life, there are a few. I did not know how to say no, so I took on too much until it started collapsing on me. I was unable to ask for help. Instead, I waited for someone to notice that I needed help and rescue me. I didn't advocate for myself, hoping instead that the contributions I made would be noticed on their own. Those are the parts of myself I am leaving behind—they are all problems that are in my power to solve. I am also leaving behind my willingness to accept platitudes that explain away gender inequality, like, "It's just the way the world works," or "That's just the way things are." Bullshit. The world may be like that, yes, but we are taking steps to change it. Don't accept the conventional wisdom if it helps maintain conventions that hold women back. If those who oppose us want platitudes, we can give them one: "Things are going to be different around here from now on."

As this chapter has shown, working so hard to fit in over the years has given us quite an arsenal of adaptive skills—we're great listeners, we're solution-oriented, we handle disappointment well, we are resourceful, we have sky-high standards for ourselves, and we work our asses off. Just imagine all the great things we can accomplish when women don't just make the world run but are running the world.

Chapter Seven

SOUND OF WOMEN'S VOICES

★

Whereas, we are the daughters of generations and generations of women throughout history whose voices were silenced, and in our own lives have either neglected to speak up or censored ourselves in an attempt to comply with conventional expectations of women's behavior;

We proclaim that to be forthright and share our best thinking with the world and honor all women, we will use our voices to speak up and we will use them to say what we truly believe.

In Homer's *Odyssey*, Telemachus, the son of Odysseus and Penelope, says to his mother, "Speech is the business of men," and then tells her to "go back to your room and take up your own work," by which he meant weaving. Granted, Penelope's weaving does prove to be critically important to the story, and Telemachus was, after all, just a teenager being rude to his mom. Nevertheless, his attitude was undoubtedly an accurate reflection of the cultural values of the time, and as Mary Beard points out in *Women and Power*, this interaction between Penelope and Telemachus is the "first recorded example [in Western literature] of a man telling a woman to 'shut up.'"[22]

Three thousand years later, women are still being told to shut up, but finally we are starting to push back. We owe it to ourselves and to all women, past and future, to continue to speak out and to refuse to be silenced.

For someone who had the job of White House communications director, I used to be surprisingly bad at cable news interviews. I would stammer and hem and haw. There were times when my appearances were so bad that my colleagues would banish me from television interviews. It was pretty humiliating. The White House communications director should be skilled and knowledgeable enough to get through a three-minute hit on a cable news channel with ease. Such interviews are not that substantive. But I made it hard on myself. The questions I was asked were, to some degree, antagonistic; that's how television interviews are often set up. The first question in particular is designed by the anchor to put you on the defensive, and I would play right into their hands. I experienced this unease most acutely in television interviews, but the same dynamics repeat themselves in any situation when a woman has to face tough questioning.

When I was asked a question by the interviewer, my instinct was to buy in to its premise. This is something you are never supposed to do in a news interview. But I would do it because I wanted the person asking the question to feel understood. I would allow that some measure of what they stated was true, just so he or she felt heard. I would do this even when the premise of their question was false. I wanted to appear reasonable and to be agreeable even when the interviewer was trying to throw me off my game. Going through all these mental gymnastics left me tongue-tied, however, and I came off as tentative; rarely would I make a declarative statement.

I am guessing this instinct of mine to please and qualify my comments will sound familiar to you. As women, we have been conditioned to please and not to be confrontational. We like to make everyone feel heard. We might repeat back a point someone else has said to buttress our own argument, in the hope that doing so will make our idea seem like something the group has come up with, not that we are pushing our own agenda. It is rare that we speak bluntly. We do not want to offend, and we certainly do not want to appear strident. We will at times avoid speaking with precision, couching our beliefs with conditional phrases like *maybe* or *I guess*. We think posing our ideas as questions instead of pronouncements will make what we have to say more palatable and less likely to be ridiculed or dismissed outright.

This tentativeness women can feel when speaking publicly did not come from nowhere—it is the result of centuries of women being punished for speaking out. The great orators of history were all men because public speaking was considered a male-only activity. As Mary Beard puts it, "Public speaking and oratory...were exclusive practices and skills that defined masculinity as a gender."[23] Indeed, if you do an online search of "great women orators," nothing comes up prior to the twentieth century. Moreover, when women opened their mouths back in the day, it was usually to nag their "henpecked" husbands. Thus women's voices were largely considered instruments of discord, and the women themselves "shrewish." Look up the term *shrew* and you'll find a long list of synonyms that paint women as relentlessly annoying and overbearing: *harpy, termagant, fury, vixen, fishwife, virago,* and *harridan.* The more synonyms there are for a word, the more commonly referred to the idea is behind the word, and thus we can see the linguistic evidence that women's voices have been dismissed as unpleasant for a very, very long time.

The idea that public speaking is the exclusive domain of men continues to have currency today. Women's voices, particularly those of women in positions of power, are still frequently described as shrill, which is no less misogynistic and insulting than being called hysterical. This bias stems from that same subconscious misogyny as the feeling expressed by Hillary detractors that "there's just something about her I don't like."

Most radio DJs are men with deep voices, and until fairly recently, all radio DJs were men, so the last few generations have been conditioned to prefer the sound of a masculine voice. As more and more women speak publicly, whether through radio work or politics or corporate lecturing, we will become more accustomed to the sound. But we can't wait for that process to play out—if we have cause to speak out, we must do it immediately, and if some people accuse us of being shrill, we need to call them out on their misogyny and continue speaking, and louder than ever.

Maria W. Stewart is believed to be the first woman in America to have given a public address on political issues in front of a mixed audience of men and women. It was in 1831 and Stewart, an African American woman, abolitionist, and early women's rights advocate, spoke out against slavery. Prior to this time, it was considered taboo for women to speak publicly in America. Stewart went on to have a short-lived public speaking career lecturing on both abolition and women's rights; she is thought to be the first woman to have her lectures printed and published in America.[24]

About the same time Stewart was making her

voice known, Lucretia Mott, an ordained Quaker minister and fervent abolitionist, shocked many men in the audience of an 1833 American Anti-Slavery Society meeting by blurting out a comment in response to something that had been said.[25] Mott's Quaker religion saw men and women as equals before God and encouraged both genders to speak freely in meetings. This was the first time she had attended one of the American Anti-Slavery Society's meetings, where women did not offer their opinions aloud. While many men were unnerved by Mott's outburst, the chairman of the meeting encouraged her to finish her comments, and Mott went on to become a very talented public speaker. Her oratory skills helped propel her and her cause of women's rights to fame. Elizabeth Cady Stanton first met Mott at an ab-olitionist gathering in London and was taken by her intellect, confidence, courage, and eloquence in advocating for abolition and women's rights, and her ability to deliver rock-solid arguments.[26] Mott's Quaker background seemed to have helped insulate her from having doubts about the worth of her opinion or concerns about the sound of her voice.

Ironically, even with Lucretia Mott's confidence

and skills and Elizabeth Cady Stanton's vision, they asked Lucretia's husband, James Mott, to chair the Seneca Falls Convention because none of the women had experience with parliamentary rules of procedure.[27] Even at the convention where the Declaration of Sentiments was approved, a man called the meeting to order and oversaw its consideration and approval. Convention protocols were unfamiliar to the women for the obvious reason that women had been denied access to political power for so long. Sadly, despite the efforts of Mott and Stanton and their sisters-in-arms, they would continue to be denied for another seventy-plus years.

Today, although there are more women executives sitting in business meetings than ever before, it's also a fact that women are more likely than men to have their assertions or ideas challenged in a meeting. A *Harvard Business Review* article noted research demonstrating that not only are men more likely than women to dominate the conversation, but the fact that women had expertise in a subject matter did not prevent them from being interrupted by men.[28] Indeed, a study by a Northwestern University law professor showed that even women as accomplished as Supreme Court justices were interrupted at significantly higher rates than male justices.[29]

The study found that male justices interrupted female justices three times as often as they did their male colleagues. The interruptions did not just come from male justices; the justices were also interrupted by *male advocates* arguing cases before the Supreme Court—yes, you read that correctly, the lawyers making arguments before the Supreme Court would actually interrupt the female justices considering their cases. In fact, in 2015, the most common form of interruptions of any justice was a male advocate interrupting Justice Sotomayor, the only woman of color on the Supreme Court. Not surprisingly, no female advocates interrupted anyone during the fifteen years in which the study was conducted, from 2002 to 2017. The analysis led the Northwestern study to conclude "that there is no point at which a woman is high-status enough to avoid being interrupted."

In another study in which men were interviewed about how they perceive women's effectiveness in meetings, more than a third of the men interviewed asserted that when female peers did speak up, they failed to articulate a strong point of view. They faulted women who "allow themselves" to be interrupted and criticized women for apologizing repeatedly and for failing to back up opinions with evidence. The men also described women as being "defensive when challenged and apt to panic or freeze if they lose attention of the room," which is hardly surprising given the way they're treated. One male CEO told these researchers, "Women are often either quiet and tentative, or they pipe up at the wrong moment, and it sounds more like noise to some of us."[30]

Speaking of noise, bropriating—the practice of men not acknowledging an idea when it is presented by a woman but lauding the same idea from a male colleague—is another phenomenon researchers working to combat gender bias in the workplace have addressed. The authors of one article noted the story of two women on a board of directors who made a pact to call it out when one of the men appropriated one of the women's idea as his own. The women found that after consistent calling out of the credit-taking, the practice stopped.[31]

I have found that calling out bropriating definitely works. It happened during the Clinton campaign—my girlfriends and I would call it out right away and, without exception, the offending man would be mortified and apologize. It even happened to Hillary, and on more than one occasion. As you can imagine, it was very awkward for those of us in the room who noticed what had just occurred. I would gently acknowledge it by saying, "Yes, I think that was the point that the secretary was making earlier." As the campaign progressed, the situation improved. Bropriating did not go away altogether, but it got better.

Despite all of our best intentions and diligence, the bias underlying the phenomenon of bropriating is very hard to extinguish altogether because even women are conditioned to pay closer attention to male speakers than female. Gender biases are deeply ingrained in each of us, and it is important to remember that no one who is on earth today is responsible for setting it in motion. As much as I get angry at the idea of women being ignored or undervalued, the point is not to assign blame but for us to end this behavior and ensure women's voices and ideas get the hearing they deserve. Being aware of the problem is the first step.

A story from early Roman times tells of the tragedy of Lucretia, a virtuous young woman who is raped by a prince. Chillingly, one of the few ways it was considered acceptable for a woman to speak publicly in those days was for her to either name someone who had attacked her or announce her own demise. Lucretia does both. She has the courage to speak up, identifying and denouncing her rapist even as she announces her own suicide—an action she must take because she has been shamed by her rapist. Ovid's *Metamorphoses* also relates the story of Philomela, another young woman who was raped—but this time, to ensure that she is not able to publicly denounce him, her rapist also cuts out Philomela's tongue. Yet even in ancient times, even in the face of this kind of violence against women who spoke up in their own defense, the men writing these stories saw enough resilience in the women around them to know that they could not be silenced entirely. Philomela, for example, may have had her tongue cut out, but she found a way to reveal her rapist by telling her story in tapestry. Both the courage of Lucretia and the resourcefulness of Philomela are evidence that, despite all the ways the world has tried to silence women through the ages, that inherent spark inside each of them that tells us women deserve better has always been there and men know it.[32]

In the fall of 2017, when the MeToo movement was really exploding, I was speaking with a friend about the impact it was having when he said, "Wow, I never realized that women went through their daily lives feeling fear." For a moment, I was speechless. "What?" I finally responded. "How is that possible?" It was a revelation to us both. He was shocked to learn that fear is a constant in the lives of women, and I was shocked to learn that he lived his daily life mostly free of it.

At some point almost every day I fear for my safety in ways the average white male never does. It wears on you, and I believe it has *shaped* us and our perceptions of the world. My friend's admission hit me like a thunderbolt. *If you don't know what it is to feel that nearly constant fear*, I thought, *of course you are able to be more confident than me. You will have the easy confidence that makes bosses think you're the right fit for the job. Of course you're going to walk the earth acting as if everything is going to work out for you. You don't have much reason to think otherwise.*

To be fair to my friend, it shook him, too, to realize that he had made it well into adulthood without appreciating just how different his life experience was from that of all the women around him. Since that time, I have thought a lot about the ways I present myself to the world, including how, despite believing myself to be a confident person, I often stammer or am uncertain about what to say. I came to appreciate that for most of my life, I have had two conversations going on in my mind at all times. The first conversation is me telling myself what I actually think. The second conversation is me checking what I actually think against how I know my views will be challenged, and then deciding if I can effectively defend what I want to say. Only after reconciling the two conversations, and after I believe I have found a way to express a thought and defend it, do I speak. If I cannot find a way to defend what I really want to say in a way that I know will be acceptable, I just don't say it. This means that for most of my life, *I have often not been saying what I actually believed*. I have been censoring myself. Most women I have shared my "two conversation" theory with agree it is something they do as well, so I believe it a common experience, but it has to end. We should always be thoughtful about what we say, but there is a huge difference between thinking before we speak and censoring ourselves from saying what we believe because we fear we will be challenged. Until we can get men to stop gratuitously challenging us, we need to stop worrying about being challenged and power through the moment with the confidence that we have something worthwhile to say.

Dear Madam President has an entire chapter dedicated to crying at work. I am a strong person, and I am also an emotional person who is easily moved to tears. It often happens that I cry at work. I am sure there are women who don't; I just don't know any of them. I argued in the book that it was time for women to disregard the stigma associated with crying at work and let the tears flow. The "crying at work" chapter ended up being one of the most popular and talked-about sections of the book. (One fifty-four-year-old woman in Seattle did a cartwheel at a book event to show me how happy it made her to be told it was okay to cry at work!) In one interview I did on the book tour, a female anchor asked me about the crying chapter and pushed me on what I would say to "those who say it is just not professional to cry at work." For a split second, I let the old two inner conversations take over. I almost responded by acknowledging that I knew there were people who might feel this way, and I understood why they might, et cetera, et cetera. But I didn't. I stopped myself. Instead I simply responded, "I say it is." The woman interviewing me paused and then gave a big smile, as if to say, *Good for you.* I think we all need to take this approach more often. Some feathers might get ruffled along the way, but confidence begets confidence, and the idea is to get to the point where I don't even hesitate the next time but just come right out with "I say it is."

The solution for me and all of us who find ourselves having that dual inner dialogue is simply to speak up more, without fear, and say what we really think. It is the only way to banish the second conversation from our minds. If the research shows men are not going to like hearing what we have to say no matter how we say it, we might as well say what we really believe. I am sure doing so will result in women drawing fire in the short term, but it is a sacrifice we must be willing to make. I know I am. When we proclaim our true voice and say what we really believe, we are effecting real change.

Chapter Eight

INSPIRE

★

Whereas, American history is dominated by the story of men and fails to adequately honor the contributions American women have made throughout the country's existence;

We proclaim that we pledge to learn and pass along the stories of courageous American women to inspire us in perpetuity.

$\mathcal{J}$udging from what I was taught in school growing up, all I needed to know about American history to prepare me for life were the stirring deeds of men. The fact that the full history of women in America remains largely unknown is a big deal. The absence of women's stories leaves a large hole in the record and means that the women who toiled on our behalf are being denied the attention they are due. But beyond that, the dearth of stories about inspiring women in our collective cultural memory affects how we view all women today.

"Where's the girl president?" At numerous events I attended with Hillary Clinton, little girls would show up with those plastic place mats that depict the American presidents, all of whom, of course, were men. The little girls were rightfully upset that there was no girl president, so they brought their place mats with them to get them signed by the woman they expected to be the first girl president. When I think of those little girls now and how bitterly disappointed they must have been with the outcome of the election, tears still well up in my eyes.

I look forward to the day when they will see a "girl president" on the place mat to model themselves after. But they shouldn't have to wait for that to happen, because there are so many women's stories that could be inspiring these girls now—stories that would help them recognize the potential in themselves and understand how much women are capable of doing. Despite the lack of mainstream coverage of the role women played in shaping our country, there is nevertheless a rich trove of stories available to us about important and courageous American women, and we need to bring them into the spotlight and make them required reading.

The history of women's suffrage in this country is well documented but only because the women involved made it a priority to record their efforts; if it had been left to the male-dominated press of the time, the movement would have been mostly forgotten. They understood the importance to history of leaving a contemporaneous account of their struggles, and thus was born the *History of Woman Suffrage* by Susan B. Anthony, Elizabeth Cady Stanton, Matilda Joslyn Gage, and Ida Husted Harper. Anthony said of the project, "Men have been faithful in noting every heroic act of their half of the race and now it should be the duty, as well as the pleasure, of women to make for future generations a record of the heroic deeds of the other half."[33]

After my experience in the 2016 campaign, I looked forward with anticipation to see how Americans would react to female candidates in the 2020 campaign. Hillary had won the popular vote, which was an encouraging sign that women should keep running. Would the women running this time be able to avoid the kind of gender bias and double standards that made Hillary's run so difficult? Not exactly. Sadly, the biases that make us more inclined to see men as leaders and be suspicious of women who seek power are still very much alive.

We judge men based on the potential we see in them and judge women based on their record of accomplishment. There is a lot of research that shows this is true whether we are considering women for a job or a promotion or elected office. One hiring simulation done in 2019 testing the appeal of male versus female job applicants found that participants valued a male's leadership *potential* more highly than his leadership *performance*.[34] The opposite was true for the women candidates that were interviewed. The female candidates were preferred over their male counterparts when they had been able to demonstrate that they had a record of leadership performance over leadership potential. The study concluded there was an *"overlooked potential effect"* that exclusively benefits men and hinders women who pursue positions that require leadership potential. In short, we trust that men will live up to expectations, but we need women to prove themselves first.

Our brains have been wired to judge men and women by different standards, and in order to rewire our thinking we must learn to be aware of our biases as they are happening, to catch ourselves before we allow an irrational, judgmental thought to overwhelm our common sense. The other part of the solution is to conscientiously learn as much as we can about the societal contributions of women in our history. The more female role models our brains can refer to, the less we will default to associating great accomplishments with men only. It is also encouraging for young women to realize that they represent a part of a continuum of female achievement.

Learning about great women of the past provides context and depth to our perceptions of female empowerment, but reading about the difficulties and resistance they faced also puts our own discomfort in perspective—if a handful of women took on the system back when women had zero rights, surely we can handle anything the opposition throws our way in the twenty-first century. Here are some accounts of women I revere and whose efforts I see reflected in the battles women undertake today.

★

Jeannette Rankin wasn't just the first woman elected to Congress. She was also on the front lines of the suffrage battle in multiple states. Born in Missoula, Montana, in 1880, she traveled to states outside her home, including New York and Washington, to help win suffrage, and eventually was part of the effort to bring that fight back to Montana. In 1914, women in Montana won the right to vote in state elections, six years before the ratification of the 19th Amendment. Jeannette Rankin won her congressional seat in 1916, later voting for a 1918 constitutional amendment providing for suffrage that Congress considered but did not pass. As Rankin said, she was "the only woman to ever vote to give women the right to vote." She was not in Congress to vote for suffrage when the 19th Amendment was finally passed a year later. Her political career stalled for the next twenty years largely due to her unpopular decision to oppose America's involvement in World War I. Like many but not all of her suffragist sisters, Rankin was a pacifist. In fact, whether or not to embrace pacifism was a point of debate and division within the suffrage movement.[35]

Before the vote, Carrie Chapman Catt, president of the National American Woman Suffrage Association (NAWSA), met with Rankin to push her to vote for war. She and many of the other leaders from NAWSA were worried that if Rankin voted against the resolution, it would damage the larger suffrage efforts by making women seem "soft" and not capable of making tough decisions like going to war. The night before the vote, Alice Paul also went to see Rankin, encouraging her to oppose the war. Paul said later about her desire for Rankin to reject the war declaration, "We thought it would be a tragedy for the first woman ever in Congress to vote for war."[36]

Rankin said of war, "You can no more win a war than you can win an earthquake." In an odd twist of fate, although she only served a total of two terms, Rankin happened to be in office when Congress voted to declare war on Japan and Germany. This time she was the only member of Congress to vote no.[37] It took an incredible amount of courage to vote against war so soon after the national trauma of Pearl Harbor, but Rankin held fast to her pacifist principles, and I admire her for her level of commitment.

Her story makes me wonder what the political situation at the time of the two world wars might have been like if women had been in power early on. Would war even have been considered an option? Would pacifism have become the norm instead of the exception? We'll never know, but I'd like to think that if Jeannette Rankin had the courage to stand alone against a Congress full of men flush with rage and nationalistic fury, then an American Congress and a British Parliament and a Japanese Diet and a German Reichstag full of women would have found a way to avoid attacking each other in the first place. In any case, Jeannette Rankin inspires me, as do the new women leaders in Congress like Ayanna Press-ley, Katie Porter, and Alexandria Ocasio-Cortez. These women are all using their seats to advocate for people largely ignored by those in power, and in that they are the direct political descendants of Jeannette Rankin.

★

Ida Wells-Barnett was an enormously accomplished and influential figure in nineteenth-century America, though her story has been underreported. Born a slave in Mississippi, she became an investigative journalist and did groundbreaking reporting on lynchings in the South during the late 1890s. Her work shed light on the depth of the problem—and it frequently put her own life in danger. She left the South and relocated to Chicago where, among other important work, she formed the Alpha Suffrage Club, the first organization to advocate for African American woman suffrage. As a suffrage leader, she traveled to Washington, DC, to be part of a parade in support of the women's vote in 1913. There was dissent about where the black women should march. Some of the white delegations from Southern states did not want to march with black women—just as with gender discrimination, racism can infect the minds of men and women with equal ease. In an effort to appease the Southern women whose political support they needed, the march organizers decided that black marchers would be placed in the back of the parade apart from the white women, but Ida Wells-Barnett refused. Even though she was not given permission to march with the other women from her state of Illinois, she did it anyway, coming out of the crowd and joining the women from her state just as the parade got under way.[38] She was fighting a war against bias on two separate fronts; that level of fearlessness and commitment to principle is tremendously inspiring, and such accounts of historical female bravery deserve the same prominence as all the stories of male heroism and fortitude we were fed as schoolchildren. If we spoke to our kids about Ida Wells-Barnett with the same reverence we reserve for Teddy Roosevelt or the Wright Brothers, they would have no choice but to conclude that women have been every bit as important as men in making this country what it is today.

★

Mary Elizabeth Quirk was born in Natick, Massachusetts, in 1871. She was a beautiful and fashionable woman with an independent spirit who worked in a millinery. She chose to wait until her late thirties to marry, and then gave birth to two children, a son, Dana, and my grandmother, Dorothy. When Mary Elizabeth was in her late forties, her husband died and she decided to open her own millinery store in Boston. She was the first woman in my family to cast a vote after women gained suffrage in 1920. She died in 1967 at the age of ninety-six. Both my grandmother and my mother have passed down to me many stories about her, and thus she has always been a source of inspiration to me. Our time on this earth only overlapped for a few months, but I have always felt a connection to her. That is my hope for all women and especially young girls—that knowing the stories of as many accomplished women as possible will give them a sense of connection with female success and provide them with a variety of achievements from which to draw inspiration.

It is crushing to consider how many stories of fearless and fascinating women have been lost to time, although I can feel their presence as I write this book. We may not know their names or their stories, but we know we belong to the same continuum of women pushing for equality. And in their anonymous honor, we should spread the fame of the extraordinary women past and present whose exploits we do know about. Their stories continue to inspire me, and I hope they inspire other women seeking to break free from the man's world. But remember, we can't expect that break to be comfortable. Challenging perceptions of what and who we find inspiring is going to be met with pushback from some quarters; often it will make us feel like we're swimming against the current. But that's what change feels like. Embrace it.

Chapter Nine

BULLY PULPIT

Whereas, we understand that the patriarchy has historically used shame and intimidation as weapons against women;

We proclaim that we will refuse to allow scare tactics to control or silence us.

𝒯hroughout recorded human history, men have used many tools to control women. Women have been subjected to physical abuse, sexual abuse, emotional abuse, legal constraints, religious traditions, withholding of rights, and so on. Progress has been made, because most of these tools are no longer available to men who still seek to control women. However, shame and intimidation remain. It is in our power to decide if we will allow men to use these weapons against us, and we proclaim that we will not.

The reckoning we see playing out before us is the result of men and women having been on a power collision course for thousands of years. By the end of the 2016 campaign, the election felt like a primal battle between those who sought to stifle the power of women and those who sought to empower them, a choice between going backward and going forward. During that fall, when it still seemed likely our side would win, a friend of Hillary's jokingly pointed out to me the irony of it taking a woman running against a misogynist to finally elect the first female president.

Her statement may ultimately prove to be true in a less immediate sense; the attempt by Trump and his allies to turn back the clock on all the progress that has been made on inequality has incensed a new generation of enlightened young women and men whose votes will decide elections for decades to come. I had hoped that the 2016 election would at least show that when given the choice between a woman and a card-carrying misogynist, America would pick the woman. And by some measurements it did, yet the man still got the power. I don't consider his win to be a lasting defeat for women, however. It just signaled the opening of a new stage in the battle between the forces protecting the patriarchy and those determined to dismantle it for the good of humankind.

I never want this battle to seem like women are pitting themselves against men—it is a shared fight for an equality that our society has already acknowledged to be logical and just. I remain optimistic about the outcome of the battle, because progress can be slowed but never stopped. Even in my own experiences, there are lessons and optimism that should empower all women to protect themselves from the shaming and blaming that men have used and continue to use to control women.

I did not know Monica Lewinsky before she came to the White House. She was assigned by the White House Internship Program to be part of our team in the White House chief of staff's office. I liked her. She worked hard, she was smart, she was diligent, and she had a good attitude. Many White House interns came from Ivy League schools and had a very high opinion of themselves. They thought they should be crafting policy and presidential speeches, not answering mail or answering phones. Monica was not like that. She was happy to pitch in and help wherever she was needed.

I was impressed by the work that she had done for our office, and I recommended her for a permanent staff job in the White House Legislative Affairs Office. She got that job. And that was the track her life was on in November 1995 when I asked her to come into the office during the government shutdown and help me answer phones in the West Wing while my boss, Leon Panetta, and other negotiators sought to reach a budget agreement with Capitol Hill that would reopen the government. Monica had not yet started her job in the Legislative Affairs Office. No new hires were going through until the shutdown had ended. That meant Monica was available to help me when I called her. It was one last task for her before she started her new job in the East Wing of the White House.

What happened next is a matter of public record. What's relevant to the story now is that one day Monica was in my life as my former intern and the next she got caught up as a pawn in an epic battle between men over power and it pretty much wrecked her life in the process. These kinds of events can impact all the women who get caught up in them. Even women who are relative bystanders like me can get caught up in the maelstrom and be made to feel responsible or complicit.

On Sunday of the Martin Luther King weekend in January 1998, I was at my desk in the White House Scheduling Office when my sister Lisa called me on my brick of a cell phone. She said she had just watched the ABC Sunday show, where a commentator said that *Newsweek* was working on a story about a former intern from Leon Panetta's office who had an affair with President Clinton.

I don't remember what I told Lisa. I quickly got off the phone and sped down the hallway to the women's bathroom and tried not to hyper-ventilate. I also tried to remember Monica's name. At that point, Monica had been gone from the White House for a few years, and it took me a few moments to recall her name. I remember playing out in my mind what might happen if it was true that she and President Clinton had had an affair and if the affair was publicly revealed. What I imagined would happen to him was pretty close to what actually ended up occurring. But I did not foresee the trauma it would cause Monica and others. This is what I saw happen.

A few days later, I watched Monica's life blow up in spectacular fashion. There are some images that stick with me from that time, like watching footage of Monica's mother leaving an interview with the FBI, crumpled over in distress. She looked physically broken. I remember being terrified for Monica after reading she was entrapped by investigators and her Pentagon colleague Linda Tripp at the Pentagon City shopping mall and then held at the nearby Ritz-Carlton for hours-long interrogation. The zeal with which the prosecutors and FBI sought to intimidate her unnerved me. In every photo Monica looked so hunted.

I myself would come home to long messages from reporters on my answering machine offering to be a sympathetic ear if I needed to vent with someone. Maybe just get coffee and talk things through. They wanted me to know that they were there for me if I needed them. In that first week,

my friend and White House colleague Doug Sos-
nik told me I needed to get a lawyer. That seemed
absurd to me, overly dramatic. I was a bit player in
all of this. Then the FBI showed up at my house
late that Friday night asking to talk to me. The
agent was actually kind to me. He understood
how scary it was to have the FBI show up at
your door. I had the presence of mind to tell him
that I would have a lawyer get in touch with him.
Doug helped me find attorney Richard Sauber,
who remains my lawyer to this day. Dick helped
me through the Starr grand jury, the Edwards
criminal trial, and the interview I had to do with
staff of the Senate Intelligence Committee about
Russia and the 2016 campaign. I like to tell Dick
that I am his favorite client. He allows that I am
his longest-standing client.

I have a distinct memory of sitting in a weird
little hallway outside the grand jury room waiting to testify in late February 1998. Dick had
brought me to the courthouse the night before so
I would be acquainted with the surroundings and
feel more comfortable. Still, I was freaked out. I
kept looking at the door leading to the grand jury
room, amazed that the "Ken Starr grand jury" I
had heard so much about actually existed in the

world in a physical form and I was getting ready to go into its hearing room and give them testimony that they hoped to use to take down the president of the United States. As we waited, Dick asked me what, if anything, I was worried about. I told him I wasn't really worried about testifying. I didn't think I knew anything of interest, but what floored me was that I had set the events in motion that might lead to the impeachment of the president. I did not blame myself. I knew that it was President Clinton's fault. But still I felt that I bore some responsibility.

The people who pursued President Clinton through the Ken Starr investigations and impeachment did not care about the welfare of Monica Lewinsky—quite the opposite. They certainly did not care about President Clinton's wife and daughter. It was all a fight about men and power, and too bad for the women who got caught in the crossfire. Bill Clinton paid a high price for his behavior, but Monica paid a far higher one. That affair has defined her life in a way it did not define President Clinton's, and it always will. It is another example of the downstream consequences for women living in a male-dominated world.

Ten years later, in August 2008, I sat in John and

Elizabeth Edwards's kitchen in Chapel Hill and tried to comfort Elizabeth as she came to terms with John's confession that he'd had an extramarital affair with Rielle Hunter. It did not seem to me that much had changed since 1998 in terms of the collateral damage women had to suffer when powerful men cheated. John Edwards had been someone I had admired and very much believed in. Needless to say, he deeply disappointed me.

John's 2008 campaign never really took off, and he dropped out of the race in late January of that year. The *National Enquirer* had reported rumors that John was having an affair earlier in the campaign cycle while he was still a candidate. He denied those reports. In the summer of 2008, *National Enquirer* was back with photos of him with a baby they said was his along with reports of a friend of John's bankrolling the raising of the baby and care of the mother. John continued to insist it wasn't true.

At that point, there was no campaign staff to help manage the press. The campaign team had long since disintegrated. I spent a lot of time with Elizabeth in those months. She had been diagnosed with terminal cancer the year before. Elizabeth very much wanted John to do an interview to say, as she hoped, that the charges were not true. I was in the position of having to tell both Elizabeth and John that I did not believe his statements that this baby was not his, and that he should not do an interview if he was going to lie.

I told them my views in private conversations. I spoke with John over the phone while I stood in my kitchen in Washington, DC. "I don't believe you," I said. It was a very hard thing to say to someone I had admired. But I was surprised to find that it also felt empowering. I was not letting myself be intimidated by someone who used to have power over me. It was not a big moment, more of a hint of the power switch that was to come in the following decade, when women finally began standing up to men in positions of power who tried to bully them.

John went ahead with the interview, where he proceeded to lie about the baby. I suppose he thought he did not have much to lose. There was a chance that the press would back off if he confessed to the affair part and leave him alone after that. I hoped for Elizabeth's sake and the sake of the whole family that he was right. I thought there was a chance that the press might decide that, while they did not believe him, he was not worth the effort of continuing to discredit his lies. But that's not what happened. His lying proved to be an accelerant for the media conflagration that was consuming him and his family. Still, I can't blame the press; John is the one who did all this.

I flew home the day after that interview and was in a bad emotional state; it was very draining trying to help Elizabeth through that time. And I was very angry with John not just for what he had done to his family but for the way he had bullied me. He was trying to exploit the sense of duty he knew I felt toward Elizabeth in wanting to make her life easier as a way to convince me to continue to help him. I told him that he could not call me anymore. If John had been my actual boss, I don't know that I would have felt empowered to do something about his manipulation. I might have had to accept it in order to keep my job, which is a common experience among women. The wonderful thing about MeToo is that it derives its clout from the sheer number of women coming forward and sharing their outrage. One woman battling a bully on her own can be incredibly daunting, but when we have each other's backs, we cannot be silenced.

On October 7, 2016, the *Access Hollywood* videotape of Donald Trump bragging about assaulting women was released. I watched it with a combination of revulsion and dread. Revulsion for what he said, and dread for what the release of this tape meant that he might do to Hillary at the debate two nights later. He would undoubtedly be unhinged. Throughout the campaign he had threatened to go after Hillary for being a "mean enabler" of her husband's infidelity. Now the moment was here. It worried me. It had worried me for the whole campaign. I just did not want Hillary to have to go through this.

He went through with his threat. He did an event prior to the debate with women who had accused Bill Clinton of assaulting them and then he brought them to the debate. He did it with the clear goal of intimidating Hillary. She was the Democratic nominee facing the Republican nominee for president on the debate stage—the biggest stage our country has. But in this case, Hillary really was just one woman facing a man trying to bully her. It happens to women every day. In the end, the moment I had dreaded ended up being a non-event because Hillary did not let it throw her. As it turns out, whether or not we let someone intimidate or shame us is our choice. Hillary did not let his power move intimidate her. Even during that bizarre few minutes when Trump started physically stalking Hillary around the stage as she spoke, she merely shook her head and plowed on, ignoring his power play and thus rendering it impotent.

A few months after the campaign, in April 2017, I ran into Monica coming out of an elevator at a hotel in Vancouver. It was the first time I had seen her in twenty years. I was glad to have the chance to tell her that I was sorry, so sorry, for all that she had to endure. It was a small gesture, but I could tell that after all the time that had passed, she appreciated hearing it.

I have learned to let go of that sense of re-sponsibility I had felt in 1998. It doesn't have anything to do with politics. It's an uneasy sense women get when we are in a bad situation and feel powerless to do anything about it. *Something bad happened on my watch. Isn't it my responsibility?* Having lived through this kind of phenomenon on a national scale was scarring. But in these past few years, I have been able to let go of this burden and see things more clearly. I know now that what happened to me was about getting caught up in a power struggle between men. I find that much of what women blame ourselves for and what we try to fix really are part of a societal phenomenon that is bigger than us. We feel powerless, but still driven to fix things. MeToo has shown us that we are not powerless and that we should never hold ourselves accountable for the things men do. After the movement exploded in the fall of 2017 with the publication of the *New York Times* story about Harvey Weinstein's sexual assaults, I knew I was witnessing a long-awaited seismic shift in the power dynamic between men and women. I have to believe it is the beginning of the end for the patriarchy.

Before, sex scandals were used by political opponents to wound other men; the impact the affair or harassment or assault had on the woman was just collateral damage that nobody cared about. MeToo flipped that. Now the women themselves are coming forward to proclaim the damage that has been done to them and demand that men be held accountable, and society is listening.

Dr. Christine Blasey Ford was one of those women. When Republican men on the Senate Judiciary Committee attempted to intimidate her into not testifying about the sexual assault she accused then Supreme Court justice nominee Brett Kavanaugh of, she refused to back down. Blasey Ford had sought an FBI investigation of her accusations prior to testifying in the confirmation hearing, so there could be an objective consideration of them before she was interrogated by partisans on the committee. The Republicans on the committee declined to wait for the FBI, presumably hoping that would scare her into not showing up. They did not want a repeat of the Anita Hill hearings, which are seared in the nation's memory as a time when a woman stood up to the powerful men who were bullying her. Their ploy did not work. Blasey Ford demanded to be heard.

There will continue to be men who resort to intimidating and shaming women. We must proclaim our determination to face down these controlling tactics wherever we encounter them, because when a woman refuses to be intimidated by a man, she takes his power away.

Chapter Ten

PARTNERS

★

Whereas, we seek to break free not from men but from our dependence on a set of male-generated systems and beliefs that hinder our advancement and result in the continued consolidation of power in men's hands;

We proclaim that men are not our opponents, but our collaborative equals, and we will work with them as partners in fulfilling all we pledge here.

$\mathcal{B}$oorish men can continue to rise to prominence in America. Let them not distract us other than to further our resolve that a world where they succeed, and women of talent and integrity fail, is not where we are meant to be.

Most men I know want better for women. They are fathers, brothers, sons, and just good people who know that it is unfair and unjust that women continue to face artificial limits on our ability to succeed. These are the men we aim to make our partners. Men often ask me what they can do to be helpful to women. Here is my advice:

It is not enough to allow women into your game. Presenting women with an opportunity to join the game without changing any of the underlying rules that determine who succeeds in a man's world is going to result in the same outcome—men will continue to rise faster than women. This is because the rules and roles in the professional world were built to suit men. For example, if you make it a priority to interview both male and female candidates for jobs, be wary if you consistently find that the men are a better fit for your organization than the women. Push yourself to consider why you think a man is a better fit and be open to the possibility that even if the woman may do the job differently than the man, she could add a new element to the work that makes it better. More of the same in the world isn't likely to help any of us.

Do not look at hiring women as "giving them an opportunity." Understand that women have something to contribute that is unique to them, just as men do. They will make your workplace better and more productive. By keeping the number of women in your company low, you aren't just being unfair to women but also robbing the world of half the population's contributions.

Don't think you have done your part for women's equality by taking the number of women on your team from 25 percent to 30 percent. Have a plan to get it to 50 percent.

Understand that the absence of overt sexism does not mean gender bias isn't at work in forming some of your views and impressions. I have to push myself every day to combat gender biases that exist in my own head. These are things all of us, men and women both, have inherited. For example, when you have concerns that a young woman is inexperienced but see a lot of promise in a similarly situated young man, you need to stop and ask yourself if you are unwittingly being influenced by gender bias. Remember, you recognize the potential in the man because you have seen his story play out successfully time and time again, but you have fewer female success stories stored in your memory for reference. Similarly, if you think a female candidate is coming across as too ambitious, try to remember that ambition is usually considered a positive in a male candidate. Push to get past your ingrained biases and allow yourself to see the same potential in a bright, young, ambitious woman as you see in a bright, young, ambitious man.

If you are going to start a new business and you default to having two white guys as partners, don't commit to that plan until you have tried to find a woman to join you. Remember, she probably has had to work twice as hard as her male counterparts to position herself to be a candidate, so you're getting a highly motivated person who doesn't let obstacles slow her down, and as such, she will make the enterprise better. This is the kind of thinking you need to incorporate into your business models in order for real equality to come about in the workplace.

For God's sake, listen to what women have to say. You are missing out on a lot of good ideas and intellectual diversity if you do not. And if you find yourself thinking that a woman is coming across as "shrill," take a step back and remember that you're hearing her through the cultural filter of thousands of years of gender bias and stereotyping. Ask yourself why the word *shrill* comes to mind in the first place and what it really means. The pitch and timbre of men's and women's voices are different, but neither is superior to the other. However, men (and women, for that matter) aren't used to hearing the voices of women in positions of power. The more we advance women up the corporate ladder, the more normal their voices will sound. In the meantime, be vigilant about hearing them as human beings trying to do their job and not as women trying to take on a man's role.

Reread the empathy exercise in chapter 2— imagining what it would be like for men if they grew up in a world where women held the vast majority of the power. This will help reorient your thinking. Another positive step is to make a concerted effort to explore and support women artists. If we push the Rock & Roll Hall of Fame to induct more women, more women will be inspired to become professional musicians.

Role models matter, and young girls need to see more examples of women succeeding in all arenas. Young boys also need to see it in order to grow up thinking that 50 percent women in any industry is the norm.

Become a fan of a women's sports team. Take your children to their games so they can see women compete, succeed, and be held up as heroes. And when women athletes are paid less, don't accept the argument that the reality of the market is that men's sports bring in more revenue. That's only true because we have been conditioned to pay attention to men's sports. In terms of what's happening on the court, a WNBA game is no less exciting than an NBA game, but we unconsciously value the latter over the former. That's what we have to change. These are the attitudes that are keeping a cap on women's success.

Don't accept a bad outcome for women as just being "the way the world is." It's the way the world has been, but we are changing it now. If you are not willing to do that, expect the same outcome: women falling dramatically short of men.

I am aware that while the vast majority of power still resides in the hands of white men, the vast majority of white men are not in positions of power. I have never assumed that most white men have it easy, and now record numbers of them are facing dwindling job opportunities in our constantly evolving economy. As we wrestle with trying to bring ancient gender imbalances into equilibrium, the thing to remember is that success is not a zero-sum game between men and women, and men do not have to give up anything in order to grant women the 50 percent responsibility for running the world that they deserve. It is also important to keep in mind that none of us created the power structure we inherited. All we can do is work together to balance things out.

Just as all women have had to learn the history of the deeds of men, you should make an effort to learn the history of women's rights. While it is replete with men who worked hard to keep women out of power, you will find there were also many who struggled alongside women in helping them win suffrage. Knowing their stories will allow you to feel like you are part of a continuum of change.

Frederick Douglass is credited with having been the voice that pushed the Seneca Falls attendees to approve the suffrage resolution Elizabeth Cady Stanton had proposed for the Declaration of

Sentiments. It was a very controversial measure. Even Lucretia Mott was uneasy that Stanton had included suffrage in the proposed resolutions. As a Quaker, she shied away from political participation in general and told Stanton that proposing suffrage would make the women in Seneca Falls look "ridiculous."[39] Stanton's own husband opposed suffrage. The measure was very much in doubt when Douglass—then the most famous black man in America—rose to speak in support of it. His remarks were not recorded, but a few days later Douglass wrote an editorial in his newspaper, *North Star*, in which he advocated for women's suffrage, arguing: "All that distinguishes man as an intelligent and accountable being is equally true of women."[40]

Obviously, it was men who cast the votes that ultimately gave women suffrage. There were no women in Congress when the 19th Amendment was approved in 1919. Jeannette Rankin served one term in the House of Representatives and had left Congress by the time the suffrage amendment was approved in the summer of 1919, although she would return twenty years later. Men also held the vast majority of seats in the state legislatures that voted to ratify the 19th Amendment.

One man, Harry Burn, played an outsize role in winning suffrage. The anti-ratification leaders in Tennessee went into the vote the morning of August 18, 1920, hopeful for a win. They thought they could count on Burn, the youngest member of the Tennessee General Assembly, to oppose ratification. And indeed, when Burn walked into the chamber to cast his vote, he wore a red rose—the flower of the antis, as those opposing ratification were called. But he also carried in his suit pocket a letter from his mother, Febb Burn, encouraging him to vote for ratification, which he did, despite the fact that his district was bitterly divided over the issue. Burn later wrote, "I believe in full suffrage as a right," and added, "I appreciated the fact that an opportunity such as seldom comes to a mortal man to free seventeen million women from political slavery was mine."[41] And thus the 19th Amendment passed by the slimmest of margins on both the national and state legislative level. If Harry's mother had not sent that letter, the push for suffrage may very well have died just as the Equal Rights Amendment did in June 1982, when ratification fell short of the requisite thirty-eight states after Congress had passed the amendment in 1972.

Fortunately, Harry Burn was a man who listened to women.

The notices announcing the Seneca Falls Convention specified that the first day of the meeting was to be for women only, but about forty men showed up along with the hundreds of women seeking admittance. The women organizing the event had a quick confab and decided that entry to the meeting would be determined by a person's attitude toward the rights of women and not their gender, and as a result, the men were let in.[42] They became partners alongside the women fighting for rights, and the support of these men was intrinsic to the ultimate success of the effort. It is a good model for the kind of backing women need and deserve from men now. It is not enough for men be morally supportive of women; you must be our active partners in this effort. The inequities that exist in the world today for women are both of our problems to solve.

Chapter Eleven

AMBITION

★

Whereas, we know that stifling our own ambition to accommodate the expectations of our male-dominated society prevents us from living up to our full potential, robs the world of our best efforts, and perpetuates the myth that ambition in a woman is an undesirable quality;

We proclaim that we will embrace and celebrate our own ambition and ambition in all women.

The Declaration of Sentiments was an audacious expression of female ambition during an era in which women simply did not question the authority of men or the unequal societal dynamic they had created. The document insisted that women be granted immediate access to rights that had been long restricted to men, cataloged the mistreatment of women throughout history, and accused men of having practiced "absolute tyranny" over them. The women who signed the document knew that they would encounter fierce opposition—the closing paragraph states, "In entering upon the great work before us, we anticipate no small amount of misconception, misrepresentation, and ridicule; but we shall use every instrumentality within our power to effect our object." They knew the negative reaction was coming because they understood that entrenched ideas cannot be challenged without provoking a counter-challenge from those who benefit from the status quo. But they believed in what they were doing and pursued their goals with a righteous determination, and we should follow their example. We are in the right, and we should never allow the fear of a backlash to deter us.

For most of my life, I would not admit to having ambition, because people always seemed to be put off by ambitious women. I was also reluctant to fully commit to my ambition—I thought the limitations of a man's world would prevent me from achieving my lofty goals, and I did not want to be disappointed. Then there was the potential for humiliation if I failed to achieve my declared ambitions, the fear that people would wonder, *Who did she think she was entertaining those ideas in the first place?* The subtext of all this was that ambition is traditionally the exclusive province of men. I decided it was safer to not express ambition at all, so I hid it, even from myself.

This is why I feel so strongly that we women have to loudly proclaim our ambition now—because stifling our ambition is not just preventing us from pursuing our dreams but also perpetuating the sense that those dreams are still out of reach for women. It seems likely that the period we are living through now will be remembered as a watershed moment in the history of female empowerment, but only if we continue to establish and maintain new models of female leadership that celebrate ambition in a woman.

Working for a female candidate for the presidency gave me constant insight into the many ways we remain uneasy with ambition in women.

For example, the oft-heard criticism that Hillary acted as if she were "entitled" to win the election always struck me as a subconscious projection of the chauvinistic belief that women are not entitled to serve as president. It was as if she were subverting the natural order of things, and it made people uncomfortable and suspicious of her. I have concluded that the only way to deal with the problem of women being disliked for having too much ambition is for them to plow through it and to fully own their ambition.

It was while working on the 2016 campaign that I first started hearing this amorphous and psychologically fraught criticism of Hillary: "There's just something about her I don't like." When voters don't like a male candidate, they always have very specific reasons for their dislike. Those reasons might not be ethically valid—say, not liking him because of his ethnicity or looks—but the specificity is always there. The nebulous criticism of Hillary was, in my opinion, all about the simple fact that she is a woman. In some cases, the people were disingenuously hiding their misogyny behind the criticism, but I think most of those who voiced this complaint really didn't understand that it was the result of their own deeply ingrained, subconscious prejudice against female leadership. It is a manifestation of our collective unease with women stepping outside the roles that they have traditionally held.

During the 2016 campaign, we met with a number of researchers and psychologists to try to understand the gender dynamics at play in the campaign. They advised us to put a lot of effort into explaining Hillary's motivations for choosing to be involved in politics and wanting to run for president. People thought she was capable of doing the job of president, but they were suspicious of her reasons for wanting the job in the first place. Can you imagine the same scrutiny being applied to a male candidate? We assume men are extremely ambitious for the highest political office in the land, and that's fine with us—in fact, we would probably have reservations about voting for a man who lacked ambition. However, a woman having the ambition to be president—and the first female president in history at that—is at odds with our traditional view of woman as communal and nurturing. To try to overcome the unease voters felt toward this ambition in a woman, we were advised to express Hillary's motivation for running for president as wanting to be "in service to others"—

as if to reassure the public that she was doing it for the most communal and nurturing of reasons. Mind you, Hillary very much has been motivated by a desire to be of service to others throughout her professional life; she wouldn't be human, however, without also wanting to experience the profound sense of personal accomplishment that comes with being elected president. But apparently, that is a luxury we only afford to male candidates for high office.

To prove that Hillary's motivations were rooted in wanting to do good in the world and not in seeking to promote herself, we talked about how the difficult childhood her mother suffered propelled Hillary to pick public service as a career and, specifically, to take her first post-law-school job with the Children's Defense Fund. We were also told that voters liked that she had been willing to work for President Obama, the man she had lost to in the 2008 primary, as his secretary of state. It was evidence to them that she was willing to put being "in service to others" over her own ambitions to be president, so we made her role in the Obama administration a key part of her biography.

Finally, we were given some advice on how to address the unique concerns some women voters had when it came to supporting women candidates. They wanted to know that the woman candidate had more experience than they did to ensure that she was capable of doing the job, but not so much more experience that they would be made to feel inferior to the woman candidate. It was not a needle we were able to thread. We saw our failure to strike this balance play out in focus groups with women voters who would point to Hillary's extraordinary accomplishments as something that alienated them. She had accomplished so much; they could never do what she did. They could not relate to her and, consequently, there was something about her they just did not like. Talk about a no-win scenario—where will we ever find a qualified female candidate for president who is relatable for women who have been prevented from following their ambitions?

In the end, nothing we did assuaged voters' concerns about Hillary's ambition, because we were trying to counter not an intellectual argument but rather a manifestation of gender bias, which is irrational and therefore immune to reason. Ultimately, there really is no way around it; we have to plow through it by refusing to compromise and by pushing back against the double standard until women feel comfortable declaring their ambition to the world. We cannot allow another generation to think it's normal to live in fear of seeming too ambitious, and we certainly can't afford to spend another election cycle shadowboxing with ourselves about whether a woman candidate is "electable." We have to dismantle these old power structures by dismantling what's in our own heads. Yes, male attitudes created those structures, but the day that women no longer feel threatened by an ambitious female leader is the day we can count on at least half the population to support her. Giving women strategies for accommodating the male chauvinists and tricking them into giving us the little they are willing to part with is not going to get the job done—on the contrary, we have to stand up and shout our ambition from the rooftops until we believe it ourselves.

Clearly, the more ambition we express and embrace, the more accepted it will become. To this end, I credit Senator Kirsten Gillibrand for running an unabashedly feminist campaign for president. It was not an anti-male campaign in any way—her argument was simply that the world would be much better off if women had a bigger role in running it. It really is not that radical a concept.

I spoke with Senator Gillibrand about her seeming fearlessness in declaring her own ambition and taking on polarizing fights. Intriguingly, she credits sports with having given her this courage. "I am not afraid to lose," she told me. As a high school and college student, she played a combination of tennis, soccer, and squash. She won some, but also lost a fair amount, and when she realized that losing wasn't the end of the world, it gave her the courage to be more competitive and aggressive about trying to win the next time. That's a lesson all women need to take to heart, because it's going to take a few "next times" before we realize our goal. But it will come.

I am often asked what advice I have for women candidates. The same advice I give them applies to all women with ambition, which is that just because someone criticizes you doesn't mean you are doing anything wrong. It's possible, of course, but if the criticism is unfounded or excessive, ignore it—don't let it get under your skin. Ignoring criticism is something many women are not comfortable doing, but when it's bias-driven, there's no point in defending yourself because you and your ambition aren't the problem.

This is something I have had to learn how to

do, because I used to accept no for an answer. If someone told me that my work wasn't good, I would automatically give their opinion more weight than my own. I eventually got over it when I learned to trust my instincts. I also learned to defend my work when I believed in it, and found that if I showed enough conviction, I was able to convince others of its value. The same principle applies to showing your ambitious side to the world—if you demonstrate enough faith in your vision, the world will eventually be convinced that you know what you're talking about. With every successful defense of ambition, we get closer to a future where we never have to defend it again.

Sojourner Truth stands out to me as one of the most inspiring examples of ambition in an American woman, the more so because she was a woman of color in a thoroughly racist era. She nearly always came up short but kept trying anyway. Having been born enslaved and sold multiple times, Truth finally escaped to freedom with her infant daughter and became an abolitionist and women's rights leader. She could not read, yet she was a nationally known lecturer. She supported herself by selling photographs of her own image, which was a novel concept at the time. In 1872, she was part of a small group of women that showed up at polling places in their hometowns demanding they be allowed to register to vote, arguing that being citizens gave them an inherent right to do so.[43] The courage it took for her to demand anything from the white establishment in 1872, let alone a right that was doubly denied her on account of both her gender and her skin color, should be an inspiration for any woman today who is hesitant to let her ambition show. Because of women like Truth, we do have the right to vote and we do have a place at the table with men—let's finish the job she started and make ambition as admirable and desirable a quality in a woman as it has been in a man since the beginning of civilized society. And when in doubt about the value of your ambition, just remember that nothing external in Sojourner Truth's life ever told her that her mind had any worth. Her self-confidence came from within, and since we still live in a world where women are undervalued, we must follow her lead and believe in ourselves until it sticks. Female ambition is something to be cele-brated, as the ever-lengthening list of accomplished women will attest. We all belong on that list.

Chapter Twelve

AGE ISN'T A NUMBER, IT'S A BADGE OF HONOR

★

Whereas, we esteem the knowledge, wisdom, and confidence women gain through life experience and know that women have important contributions to make at each stage of their lives;

We proclaim that we value women of all ages.

$\mathcal{W}$hen I turned forty-four years old, I went out to a birthday lunch with a friend who was about ten years older than me. This woman had held very senior jobs in politics and was in what I considered to be the middle—not the end—of a very successful career. She advised me that I ought to leave the Washington, DC, think tank I was working for and go off to start my own public relations firm. "This town is hard for women over fifty," she said to me. "It just is. You need to start building something on your own now while you are still in your forties."

It was a distressing thing to hear from a woman I admired and looked to as a role model. I absorbed all that went unsaid in her warning to me: I had to start a business while I was still in my forties and potential clients saw something of value in me. Once I was past fifty, the opportunities I had enjoyed in life would dissipate; I would be considered washed up. Embedded deeper in her words was a more chilling message about how the man's world viewed women: *Women over fifty are too old to be attractive, too old to be diverting enough for men to want to have us around in their world.* It was as if we had been merely objects for their amusement all along, and once we lost our youth, men would evict us from the spot we never belonged to in the first place, and probably replace us with a new generation of unsuspecting young women.

It goes without saying that she would not have needed to give the same warning to a man in Washington, DC. It is true that society puts a premium on youth for both men and women, and plenty of men have suffered the consequences of ageism. But there's no question that it hits women harder, partly because a woman's physical appearance is often more of an issue in the workplace than it is for her male co-workers, and partly because our male-dominated society is still laboring under the sexist notion that women don't age as well as men do. In DC, older men are often revered as wise—we affectionately refer to them as graybeards in politics. They are men who have decades of experience in politics and, in many cases, have served as advisers to multiple presidents. Their experience gives them the ability to offer sage advice, as I believe my experience does. But the message I was being sent was that age and experience were not valued in women, and that I should make hay while I was still young enough to be salable in this man's world. Of all the illogical premises behind gender inequality in the professional world, none gets me more riled up than this one. Women who have been around for a while and have experienced a lot are survivors—they represent an extremely valuable resource, and discarding them before their time is a shameful waste.

I do not mean to sound ungrateful to this woman. She was my friend; she was trying to warn me about the difficulties I was going to face in the next stage of my life. It was the kind of advice our group of women friends had been giving to each other over the years: "Hey, here's what you need to say in that meeting so the guys think you are one of them." "Be careful of that woman over there. She is not a sister. She is out for herself." This heads-up was just another piece of guidance meant to let me know of the next accommodation I was going to have to make to survive in a man's world. But I found it was one I was unwilling to make.

While her words initially unnerved me, I somehow knew that they would not apply to me. I could not see clearly what my post-fifty future was to be, but I knew it was not going to be what she described. I just had too much faith in myself. Eventually the unease I felt about her comments was replaced by anger. *This town is hard for women over fifty. It just is,* I thought. *Then fuck this town.* The women I know who are over fifty have a ton to contribute, and the men I know and whose opinions I respect understand that about women, too. They understand that anything holding women back robs everyone of the best the world can be. And they embrace the obvious truth that age enhances, not diminishes, a woman's abilities.

I felt like I had a lot to contribute as a young woman, too. I spent my late twenties and early thirties working in relatively junior jobs in President Bill Clinton's White House. I was thrilled to be in the West Wing of the White House, but felt like I was capable of so much more than I was doing at the time. A reporter whom I was friendly with described me as "coltish." Although that term as applied to women probably originated in the mind of a sexist male, there was some truth in what he said. I could be overexuberant, full of potential but shaky. I would buck with frustration. I was quite certain in my capabilities, but less certain about what the world would permit me to do. It made me think I had to grab what I could before a window closed on me. I also felt like I had more strength and power in me than the world or I knew what to do with; I felt gangly with strength.

A Pat Benatar lyric rattled around in my mind: "Maybe I just wouldn't know what to do with my strength anyway." Looking back now, I see that I was anxious because I felt I was operating under a ticking clock. I only had so much time to prove myself before time ran out on me.

I was recently comparing notes about the time pressures on women with a female friend who is an artist. She is in her late forties and feels like she is just beginning to enter the most productive time of her career. She has always known that she had a great deal of talent in her but needed the knowledge and experience that came with age before she could realize her full potential. I feel the same way about my own work. I am fifty-three years old and believe I am doing the best work of my career. I love being this age; it has turned out to be the most exhilarating time of my life. Since I first entered the workplace, I have spent twelve years working in the White House, been a part of five presidential campaigns, written a book, and paid close attention all along the way to what those experiences and the ones I had with my own family and friends could teach me about life. All of what I lived and absorbed has inculcated in me a unique body of wisdom, and I am lucky to be in a position to put it to use. I know many women who came before me were not as fortunate and found themselves sidelined and their informed perspectives only occasionally tapped by friends or family. So much of this accumulated wisdom has been lost to posterity, but, as our proclamation makes clear, we will no longer sit back and allow this to happen unchallenged.

What I have lost to the years are mostly the things that used to hold me back. For example, I have left behind a lot of doubt and insecurities. Ironically, with the passing of time, I feel like I am in less of a rush. I no longer have that sense that a window is getting ready to shut on me. I have enough experience with myself to trust myself. If something is important enough for me to really want to do, I know I will be able to rise to the occasion to get it done. Most significantly for my peace of mind, I have largely been able to shed an emotion that can rob so much life from you if you let it: dread. I used to waste a lot of energy on dread—worrying about silly things at work and big things like how I would face each phase of the demise of my sister. What I found out about myself—about all of us—is that we are all stronger than we know. We are strong enough to get through any moment. I have come to trust that I will know how to handle what life throws my way, which is enormously freeing. It's one of the gifts of age. I share this with you to tell you that it can all be possible for you, too. If you are my age or older, you know what I am talking about. If you are younger than me, I want you to know that your best days are ahead of you—truly.

In reviewing what I have lost, I find that losing the rosy glow of youth does not bother me like I thought it would. We put so much value into how women look, and apart from being a shallow perspective, it also distracts us from the many other qualities of worth women possess. I actually like the lines on my face and on the faces of other women my age. They tell us a lot about the lives we have led. I have always found them a comfort. So I let my lines be. I still color my hair—over the course of my lifetime, most women have been so careful not to let the world see their hair turn gray that my own perception of what is attractive is still affected by it. I have not found it in myself to embrace the gray, not yet anyway, but I admire the women who do. To me, these women exude confidence. I see their gray hair as the same indicator of experience and ability that it is for older men.

For now, I think women should do whatever they want with their faces and their hair. We should wear whatever clothes we like, too. From what I have observed in my own life and in reading history, society is not going to get over its obsession with women's appearance anytime soon. When Jeannette Rankin was elected as the first woman to Congress, there was nationwide speculation about what this upstart woman might wear when she got to the House of Representatives. On her first day in Congress, the *Washington Post* ran a story about her attire under the headline "Congresswoman Rankin Real Girl; Likes Nice Gowns and Tidy Hair." During her election, the *New York Times* commented on her "wealth of red hair," noting that nothing was "more beautiful than her red hair." One hundred years later, the press continues to focus on the hair and wardrobe of women in the public eye, particularly those in politics. For the foreseeable future, we are going to be judged on our appearance more heavily than men are, no matter what we do. So let's present ourselves to the world however we want and worry only about pleasing ourselves when standing in front of the mirror.

My life is not perfect. It continues to contain

disappointment and heartbreak because they are part of the human condition. But I find that I am better equipped to deal with life now and to get the most out of it. Gloria Steinem has said that women grow more radical with age, while men become more conservative. She sees women's lack of power as pushing them in that direction as they grow older. I would not describe the transformations I have made as becoming more radical; I just see things more clearly. There are so many conflicting signals women are sent in our lives about who we are supposed to be and what we can expect for ourselves that it fogs our view of the world. As I have grown older, the fog has dissipated. What I see now is that the man's world has put intolerable constraints on women, and we have to break from it. It is not radical; it is simply true.

I find that the "colt" I used to be has turned into a thoroughbred. I am less inclined to buck with frustration. I finally feel like I have gained enough knowledge and skill to match the potential I've always had in me. I want to proclaim my age from the rooftops, proclaim the truth that women get better with age. I also find that I no longer struggle with what to do with my strength and power. I know how to use it for good.

Part of what I use my power for is to make sure younger women's voices are heard and respected. I learn a lot from the younger women in my life, whether they are my stepdaughters, nieces, friends, or colleagues. In meetings, the young women I work with are often the ones least likely to speak up and the ones I find have the most interesting perspectives to share. Women who are in their twenties now grew up in a very different, and in many ways darker, world than I did. They have little recollection of a world before 9/11 or the Columbine school shooting or the Great Recession. I find their different life experience means they are often more strident in their views than I was at their age, more likely to favor bolder solutions, and more likely to take risks. They are impatient about women's lot in life, too. I like this about them. Women need to be impatient. I may be doing the best work of my career, but it does not mean I can't still learn. I learn a lot by listening to these women.

The last time women banded together and secured the big win of suffrage, women of all ages were part of the movement that made it happen. There were young, impatient women like Alice Paul and her compatriots who led the more radical wing of the movement, as well as women in their sixties like Carrie Chapman Catt who headed the more establishment wing and helped oversee the Tennessee ratification that put suffrage over the top. You needed the full spectrum of women engaged in the fight to win. We do now, too. In 2018, women were elected in their twenties, thirties, forties, fifties, sixties, and seventies, and we all know we have something to contribute regardless of age. And if you ever have any questions about whether women get better with age and what more you might have to contribute in your older years, take a look at Speaker Nancy Pelosi. She did not run for office until she was forty-seven years old. She became the first woman Speaker at age sixty-six and again at age seventy-eight. And in my view, she gets even more skilled as she gets older. We should all recognize our capacity to contribute at every age and feel the obligation to do so because the world needs our perspective. No one looks at the world today and thinks that we have it all figured out. We need more perspectives, more voices from women of all ages to speak up.

Therefore, there will be no more clocks on women's worth. That's a vestige of the man's world. I don't feel the need to rush, to grab what I want before it is denied to me forever. I am content to let it unfold, secure in the knowledge that I now know what I need to be successful on my own. The trappings I used to chase in the man's world no longer interest me, and I do not follow their rules.

I proclaim that my age and experience are assets to me. I proclaim that my experience gives me value and potential. It means I know best how to use my skills to make a difference in the world. I proclaim that my best work still lies ahead.

Chapter Thirteen

A WOMAN'S VALUE

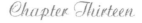

We proclaim that we will be the change we seek in the world by demonstrating in both word and deed that we value and celebrate the efforts of all women to the same extent that we value and celebrate the efforts of men.

*W*hen I was a child, I was baffled by the notion that women were the weaker sex. It was such a blatantly false claim that I never believed it. I only had to look at my own mother to know it was not true. My mother is so strong that some part of me has always believed her to be indestructible. Nor did I accept that men were physically stronger than women. Women's bodies can give birth, and nothing is more powerful than that.

I saw that women were wise, too. They grew up understanding they would not have the same opportunities men did to determine their own course in life. They knew women were dependent on others for survival and had to live with the consequences of decisions other people made on their behalf. From what I could glean watching them, women did not know much about life's possibilities, but they knew a lot about life's reality. Not distracted by visions of the ideal just over the horizon, women were the ones who really understood reality, because it was their lot all day every day.

History gave us detailed accounts of the sufferings of famous men over the years, but the tribulations of women were left to the imagination. However, having witnessed female hardship in my own time, I can imagine plenty. Women were the ones who dealt with the real grit of life. They had to be tougher than the men. Since they did not have a profession outside the home that gave them an escape, they did not have the luxury of looking away when life got hard. They had to deal with the heartbreaks, the illnesses, and the disappointments without any breaks.

These were all things I intuited about women growing up. I also absorbed all the lessons that told me men were more interesting and held the power, but I knew the reality was more complicated than that. Power is a possession men hold. The way I saw it, power might be something men *have*, but powerful is what women *are*.

However, I could see that despite all the strength, wisdom, and power women had, they were not valued as much as men. That is the fundamental premise of the man's world, and it is this counterintuitive belief we have to upend. We have to believe more in ourselves than in any long-accepted concepts of gender value, and we have to consistently and demonstratively value women the same as men. This means guarding against all the subtle verbal and behavioral clues that drive our subconscious assent to systemic gender inequality. It means paying close attention to things we are used to ignoring, and it means proactively supporting equal female participation at all levels of government and industry.

Demonstrating that we value women as much as men means we pay women the same as men for the same work—period. This is such a straightforward, fair, and equitable position that it embarrasses me to have to insist on it. But the wheels of positive change for women turn very slowly in the man's world, which is why we have to move things forward ourselves. Also, men have been accumulating wealth for its own sake, and have been widely respected and admired for doing so, for thousands of years. So when ambitious women are paid big bucks, let's applaud the accomplishment.

Equal value means we listen as eagerly and respectfully to what women have to say as we do for men. It means we value the skills women have developed in the workplace to get things done by promoting them as rapidly as men with the same qualifications. It means we embrace women's ambition because we want them to contribute their best work to the world by being uninhibited in their quest to accomplish. It means we value mothers as mothers, and ensure they finally have the support they need in and out of the work-place, like every other developed nation on the planet. It means we value and support women's art, literature, music, and film with the same vigor as that of their male counterparts, which in turn means giving unknown women artists, writers, musicians, and filmmakers a chance and spread-ing the word if we genuinely like their stuff. It means we value and continue to be inspired by the history of women's struggles and acknowledge the importance of promoting positive and accom-plished role models, past, present, and future, for girls to emulate. Finally, it means that we appreci-ate the value of our own individual efforts and the impact they can have in seeking the gains we want for women in the world. We women consistently discount the power of our own voices and actions to effect change. We have the power to change the world by changing how we engage in it.

We should all be proud to be part of a long line of women who have struggled throughout his-tory for equality. We should also remember that continued progress for women is not guaranteed. Complacency has always been our worst enemy, and now, in the shadow of right-wing threats to progressive milestones, we must guard against it more vigilantly than ever before.

We are the women who have to finish the job. We have to commit to adhering to all we have proclaimed here. We won't be placated by small gains for women; we know equality for women means we are valued the same as men and won't be satisfied till we achieve parity. We will support other women because we know that if the patriarchal forces that still exist in the world stop one woman, they gain ground on us all. We will support other women because we are all sisters and need to have each other's backs, just as men have looked out for one another since time immemorial. We will reject the idea that we are in zero-sum competition with other women for success. We will speak up and say what we truly believe. We will remember that our voices have the power to change the world.

We will make men our partners in this endeavor because we know that they, too, want a world where both men and women flourish. We are declaring our independence from the man's world as it currently exists and creating a new world where women and men have the same opportunities to succeed. We know there is no value to anyone—

men included—in maintaining a world where so many are disadvantaged and hence where so much time and effort must be taken up with trying to level the playing field, and where so much talent is therefore going to waste. These are the core beliefs of our Declaration of Independence.

The new generation of women and young girls coming up in the world now inspires me and makes me hopeful. So many girls enter adulthood these days with a level of strength and inherent belief in themselves that took many of us forty years to attain. They are full of joy and potential, but they can still become inhibited by exposure to the man's world—it is still capable of convincing us we have to change ourselves to fit in. It makes us doubt ourselves, censor ourselves, stifle our ambition. It is not who women really are.

Imagine what the little girls growing up in the world today will be able to achieve if we break the cycle of gender submission once and for all. That is the gift we can give ourselves and them—a future free of the biases that have held us back for so long. We can make the next important chapter of American history the one where women break with their old complacent ways and band together to finally realize the golden promise of equality.

Let us proclaim all of this, and always believe in ourselves and our abilities—in honor of all the women who came before us, in honor of all the women making their way in the world today, and in honor of the unbridled women achievers of the future, for whom the sky will be the limit.

DECLARATION OF INDEPENDENCE FROM A MAN'S WORLD

*W*hen, in the course of human events, it becomes necessary for people to dissolve a set of beliefs, biases, and behaviors that fail to recognize the inherent value of one half of the population and perpetuate impediments to achieving all that their God-given rights and talents entitle them to, respect for the opinions of all requires that they should declare the causes that impel them to take such a course and the rights to which they are entitled.

We hold these truths to be self-evident:

That all people are created equal; that they are endowed by their Creator with certain unalienable rights; that among these are life, liberty, and the pursuit of happiness; that the disenfranchisement of women and all people of color at the country's founding continues to have significant negative consequences on these populations today; that human beings are more inclined to suffer, while evils are sufferable, than to right themselves by abolishing the forms to which they are accustomed. But when a long train of abuses and usurpations, pursuing the same object, evinces a design to keep the female half of the population in a state of sub-conscious servitude, it is their right, it is their duty, to throw off the fetters that have hindered their progress and to provide new guards for their future security and fulfillment. Such has been the patient sufferance of women that fully one hundred years after suffrage was introduced in America, they continue to live in a world where they are under-valued and grossly underrepresented in positions of power relative to men; that in the face of this stagnation for women, they have no choice but to declare their independence from a man's world. Therefore, we hereby proclaim the following:

- We will be the change we seek in the world by demonstrating in both word and deed that we value and celebrate the efforts of all women to the same extent that we value and celebrate the efforts of men.

- We refuse to contribute to the stagnation of women's progress by believing there to be a limited number of women that can succeed in the world. We reject the societally implied notion that the professional advancement of women is a zero-sum game, and we hereby acknowledge that the opportunities for women to succeed are in fact infinite.

- We will support other women because they are our sisters. We know that when we unite to support each other women succeed, and when we are divided we perpetuate our own second-class status.

- We will no longer be placated by token gestures that do not lead to substantive progress toward equality for women. We know that being satisfied with the incremental allowance of small gains for women helps perpetuate power systems that have stifled women throughout history.

- To achieve the higher standard of performance women have had to meet relative to our male colleagues, we have often worked harder than men and adapted our behavior to be accepted in a man's world. We pledge to embrace those skills we have developed that serve us well and make us effective and shed the behaviors that we determine to be self-defeating for women.

- We will say what we believe, even when we know it is not what a woman is expected to say. We do this to be forthright and to share our best thinking with the world. We do this to honor ourselves, to honor the generations of women who came before whose voices were silenced, and to honor the generations of women to come.

- We know that American history is dominated by the story of men and fails to adequately honor the contributions American women have made throughout the country's existence. We pledge to learn and pass along the stories of courageous American women to inspire us in perpetuity.

- We understand that the patriarchy has historically used shame and intimidation as weapons against women, and we refuse to allow these scare tactics to control or silence us.

- Men are not our opponents, but our collaborative equals, and we will work with them as partners in fulfilling all we pledge here. We seek to break free not from men but from our dependence on a set of male-generated systems and beliefs that hinder our advancement and result in the continued consolidation of power in men's hands.

- We embrace and celebrate our ambition and ambition in all women. We know that stifling our own ambition to accommodate the expectations of our male-dominated society prevents us from living up to our full potential, robs the world of our best efforts, and perpetuates the myth that ambition in a woman is an undesirable quality.

- We value women of all ages. We esteem the knowledge, wisdom, and confidence women gain through life experience and know that women have important contributions to make at each stage of their lives.

We, therefore, the women of the United States of America, with confidence in our ability, certainty of our worth, and devotion to each other, pledge to uphold all we proclaim here to realize the potential in each of us and help fulfill America's promise of equality for all.

★

DECLARATION OF SENTIMENTS

July 20, 1848

When, in the course of human events, it becomes necessary for one portion of the family of man to assume among the people of the earth a position different from that which they have hitherto occupied, but one to which the laws of nature and of nature's God entitle them, a decent respect to the opinions of mankind requires that they should declare the causes that impel them to such a course.

We hold these truths to be self-evident; that all men and women are created equal; that they are endowed by their Creator with certain inalienable rights; that among these are life, liberty, and the pursuit of happiness; that to secure these rights governments are instituted, deriving their just powers from the consent of the governed. Whenever any form of Government becomes destructive of these ends, it is the right of those who suffer from it to refuse allegiance to it, and to insist upon the institution of a new government, laying its foundation on such principles, and organizing its powers in such form as to them shall seem most likely to effect their safety and happiness. Prudence, indeed, will dictate that governments long established should not be changed for light and transient causes; and accordingly, all experience hath shown that mankind are more disposed to suffer, while evils are sufferable, than to right themselves, by abolishing the forms to which they were accustomed. But when a long train of abuses and usurpations, pursuing invariably the same object, evinces a design to reduce them under absolute despotism, it is their duty to throw off such government, and to provide new guards for their future security. Such has been the patient sufferance of the women under this government, and such is now the necessity which constrains them to demand the equal station to which they are entitled.

The history of mankind is a history of repeated injuries and usurpations on the part of man toward woman, having in direct object the establishment of an absolute tyranny over her. To prove this, let facts be submitted to a candid world.

He has never permitted her to exercise her inalienable right to the elective franchise.

He has compelled her to submit to laws, in the formation of which she had no voice.

He has withheld from her rights which are given to the most ignorant and degraded men—both natives and foreigners.

Having deprived her of this first right as a citizen, the elective franchise, thereby leaving her without representation in the halls of legislation, he has oppressed her on all sides.

He has made her, if married, in the eye of the law, civilly dead.

He has taken from her all right in property, even to the wages she earns.

He has made her, morally, an irresponsible being, as she can commit many crimes, with impunity, provided they be done in the presence of her husband. In the covenant of marriage, she is compelled to promise obedience to her husband, he becoming, to all intents and purposes, her master—the law giving him power to deprive her of her liberty, and to administer chastisement.

He has so framed the laws of divorce, as to what shall be the proper causes of divorce; in case of separation, to whom the guardianship of the children shall be given, as to be wholly regardless of the happiness of women—the law, in all cases, going upon a false supposition of the supremacy of man, and giving all power into his hands.

After depriving her of all rights as a married woman, if single and the owner of property, he has taxed her to support a government which recognizes her only when her property can be made profitable to it.

He has monopolized nearly all the profitable employments, and from those she is permitted to follow, she receives but a scanty remuneration.

He closes against her all the avenues to wealth and distinction, which he considers most honorable to himself. As a teacher of theology, medicine, or law, she is not known.

He has denied her the facilities for obtaining a thorough education—all colleges being closed against her.

He allows her in Church as well as State, but a subordinate position, claiming Apostolic authority for her exclusion from the ministry, and with some exceptions, from any public participation in the affairs of the Church.

He has created a false public sentiment, by giving to the world a different code of morals for men and women, by which moral delinquencies which exclude women from society, are not only tolerated but deemed of little account in man.

He has usurped the prerogative of Jehovah himself, claiming it as his right to assign for her a sphere of action, when that belongs to her conscience and her God.

He has endeavored, in every way that he could to destroy her confidence in her own powers, to lessen her self-respect, and to make her willing to lead a dependent and abject life.

Now, in view of this entire disfranchisement of one-half the people of this country, their social and religious degradation,—in view of the unjust laws above mentioned, and because women do feel themselves aggrieved, oppressed, and fraudulently deprived of their most sacred rights, we insist that they have immediate admission to all the rights and privileges which belong to them as citizens of these United States.

In entering upon the great work before us,

we anticipate no small amount of misconception, misrepresentation, and ridicule; but we shall use every instrumentality within our power to effect our object. We shall employ agents, circulate tracts, petition the State and national Legislatures, and endeavor to enlist the pulpit and the press in our behalf. We hope this Convention will be followed by a series of Conventions, embracing every part of the country.

Firmly relying upon the final triumph of the Right and the True, we do this day affix our signatures to this declaration.

★

DECLARATION OF INDEPENDENCE

In Congress, July 4, 1776.

The unanimous Declaration of the thirteen united States of America, When in the Course of human events, it becomes necessary for one people to dissolve the political bands which have connected them with another, and to assume among the powers of the earth, the separate and equal station to which the Laws of Nature and of Nature's God entitle them, a decent respect to the opinions of mankind requires that they should declare the causes which impel them to the separation.

We hold these truths to be self-evident, that all men are created equal, that they are endowed by their Creator with certain unalienable Rights, that among these are Life, Liberty and the pursuit of Happiness.—That to secure these rights, Governments are instituted among Men, deriving their just powers from the consent of the governed, — That whenever any Form of Government becomes destructive of these ends, it is the Right of the People to alter or to abolish it, and to institute new Government, laying its foundation on such principles and organizing its powers in such form, as to them shall seem most likely to effect their Safety and Happiness. Prudence, indeed, will dictate that Governments long established should not be changed for light and transient causes; and accordingly all experience hath shewn, that mankind are more disposed to suffer, while evils are sufferable, than to right themselves by abolishing the forms to which they are accustomed. But when a long train of abuses and usurpations, pursuing invariably the same Object evinces a design to reduce them under absolute Despotism, it is their right, it is their duty, to throw off such Government, and to provide new Guards for their future security.—Such has been the patient sufferance of these Colonies; and such is now the necessity which constrains them to alter their former Systems of Government. The history of the present King of Great Britain is a history of repeated injuries and usurpations, all having in direct object the establishment of an absolute Tyranny over these States. To prove this, let Facts be submitted to a candid world.

He has refused his Assent to Laws, the most wholesome and necessary for the public good.

He has forbidden his Governors to pass Laws of immediate and pressing importance, unless suspended in their operation till his Assent should be obtained; and when so suspended, he has utterly neglected to attend to them.

He has refused to pass other Laws for the accommodation of large districts of people, unless those people would relinquish the right of Representation in the Legislature, a right inestimable to them and formidable to tyrants only.

He has called together legislative bodies at

places unusual, uncomfortable, and distant from the depository of their public Records, for the sole purpose of fatiguing them into compliance with his measures.

He has dissolved Representative Houses repeatedly, for opposing with manly firmness his invasions on the rights of the people.

He has refused for a long time, after such dissolutions, to cause others to be elected; whereby the Legislative powers, incapable of Annihilation, have returned to the People at large for their exercise; the State remaining in the mean time exposed to all the dangers of invasion from without, and convulsions within.

He has endeavoured to prevent the population of these States; for that purpose obstructing the Laws for Naturalization of Foreigners; refusing to pass others to encourage their migrations hither, and raising the conditions of new Appropriations of Lands.

He has obstructed the Administration of Justice, by refusing his Assent to Laws for establishing Judiciary powers.

He has made Judges dependent on his Will alone, for the tenure of their offices, and the amount and payment of their salaries.

He has erected a multitude of New Offices, and sent hither swarms of Officers to harrass our people, and eat out their substance.

He has kept among us, in times of peace, Standing Armies without the Consent of our legislatures.

He has affected to render the Military independent of and superior to the Civil power.

He has combined with others to subject us to a jurisdiction foreign to our constitution, and unacknowledged by our laws; giving his Assent to their Acts of pretended Legislation:

For Quartering large bodies of armed troops among us:

For protecting them, by a mock Trial, from punishment for any Murders which they should commit on the Inhabitants of these States:

For cutting off our Trade with all parts of the world:

For imposing Taxes on us without our Consent:

For depriving us in many cases, of the benefits of Trial by Jury:

For transporting us beyond Seas to be tried for pretended offences

For abolishing the free System of English Laws in a neighbouring Province, establishing therein an Arbitrary government, and enlarging its Boundaries so as to render it at once an example and fit instrument for introducing the same absolute rule into these Colonies:

For taking away our Charters, abolishing our most valuable Laws, and altering fundamentally the Forms of our Governments:

For suspending our own Legislatures, and declaring themselves invested with power to legislate for us in all cases whatsoever.

He has abdicated Government here, by declaring us out of his Protection and waging War against us.

He has plundered our seas, ravaged our Coasts, burnt our towns, and destroyed the lives of our people.

He is at this time transporting large Armies of foreign Mercenaries to compleat the works of death, desolation and tyranny, already begun with circumstances of Cruelty & perfidy scarcely paralleled in the most barbarous ages, and totally unworthy the Head of a civilized nation.

He has constrained our fellow Citizens taken Captive on the high Seas to bear Arms against their Country, to become the executioners of their friends and Brethren, or to fall themselves by their Hands.

He has excited domestic insurrections amongst

us, and has endeavoured to bring on the inhabitants of our frontiers, the merciless Indian Savages, whose known rule of warfare, is an undistinguished destruction of all ages, sexes and conditions.

In every stage of these Oppressions We have Petitioned for Redress in the most humble terms: Our repeated Petitions have been answered only by repeated injury. A Prince whose character is thus marked by every act which may define a Tyrant, is unfit to be the ruler of a free people.

Nor have We been wanting in attentions to our Brittish brethren. We have warned them from time to time of attempts by their legislature to extend an unwarrantable jurisdiction over us. We have reminded them of the circumstances of our emigration and settlement here. We have appealed to their native justice and magnanimity, and we have conjured them by the ties of our common kindred to disavow these usurpations, which, would inevitably interrupt our connections and correspondence. They too have been deaf to the voice of justice and of consanguinity. We must, therefore, acquiesce in the necessity, which denounces our Separation, and hold them, as we hold the rest of mankind, Enemies in War, in Peace Friends.

We, therefore, the Representatives of the united

States of America, in General Congress, Assembled, appealing to the Supreme Judge of the world for the rectitude of our intentions, do, in the Name, and by Authority of the good People of these Colonies, solemnly publish and declare, That these United Colonies are, and of Right ought to be Free and Independent States; that they are Absolved from all Allegiance to the British Crown, and that all political connection between them and the State of Great Britain, is and ought to be totally dissolved; and that as Free and Independent States, they have full Power to levy War, conclude Peace, contract Alliances, establish Commerce, and to do all other Acts and Things which Independent States may of right do. And for the support of this Declaration, with a firm reliance on the protection of divine Providence, we mutually pledge to each other our Lives, our Fortunes and our sacred Honor.

ACKNOWLEDGMENTS

True to the spirit of this book, I am a woman who has been generously supported by other women in undertaking this project. First among them is my editor, Gretchen Young, who was an unflagging partner throughout the writing process and whose sharp insights made this a far better book. I am very indebted to her. Barbara Lee and Amanda Hunter of the Barbara Lee Foundation do important work studying and finding ways to combat gender bias on behalf of women candidates and helped me think through some of the themes of this book. Many women in Missoula, including State Senator Diane Sands, Carol Williams, and Whitney Williams were generous in sharing their time and knowledge of Montana's women's history. It was Ann Tickle of Bristol, Tennessee, who was the first to tell me of *The Woman's Hour* and the history-making drama that unfolded in Nashville in August 1920, and Hannah Gadsby generously gave me a copy of Mary Beard's *Women and Power*.

I am also grateful for the work done by American University's Women and Politics Institute headed by Betsy Fischer Martin. Finally, I am lucky to have a great man in my life, my husband, Jim Lyons. I could not do this kind of work without his support and love. He sustains me.

NOTES

1 Angela Dobson, *Remember the Ladies: Celebrating Those Who Fought for Freedom at the Ballot Box* (New York and Nashville: Center Street Hachette Book Group, 2017), 84–96.

2 American Express, "The 2018 State of Women-Owned Businesses Report," 2018, https://about.americanexpress.com/files/doc_library/file/2018-state-of-women-owned-businesses-report.pdf.

3 Judith Warner, Nora Ellmann, and Diana Boesch, "The Women's Leadership Gap: Women's Leadership by the Numbers," Center for American Progress, November 20, 2018, https://cdn.americanprogress.org/content/uploads/2018/11/19121654/WomensLeadershipFactSheet.pdf.

4 Claire Cain Miller, Kevin Quealy, and Margot Sanger-Katz, "The Top Jobs Where Women Are Outnumbered by Men Named John," *New York Times*, April 24, 2018, https://www.nytimes.com/interactive

/2018/04/24/upshot/women-and-men-named
-john.html.

5 Dobson, *Remember the Ladies*, 86–101.

6 Estelle Freedman, *No Turning Back: The History of Feminism and the Future of Women* (New York: Ballantine Books, 2002), 45–72.

7 Freedman, *No Turning Back*, 51–52.

8 Winifred Conkling, *Votes for Women: American Suffragists and the Battle for the Ballot* (Chapel Hill, NC: Algonquin, 2018), 165–82.

9 Pew Research Center, "Wide Partisan Gaps in the US Over How Far the Country Has Come on Gender Equality," October 18, 2017, https://www.pewsocialtrends.org/2017/10/18/wide-partisan-gaps-in-u-s-over-how-far-the-country-has-come-on-gender-equality.

10 World Economic Forum, "The Global Gender Gap Report 2018," December 17, 2018, https://www.weforum.org/reports/the-global-gender-gap-report-2018.

11 McKinsey & Company, "Women in the Workplace 2019," October 2019, https://www.mckinsey.com/featured-insights/gender-equality/women-in-the-workplace-2019.

12 Warner, Ellmann, and Boesch, "The Women's Leadership Gap."

13 Rosabeth Moss Kanter, "Some Effect of Proportion on Group Life: Skewed Sex Ratios

and Responses to Token Women," *American Journal of Sociology* 82 (1977).

14 LinkedIn Economic Graph, "World Economic Forum's the Global Gender Gap Report," December 19, 2017, https://economicgraph .linkedin.com/research/world-economic-forums -the-global-gender-gap-report-2017.

15 Dobson, *Remember the Ladies*, 236–40.

16 Jane J. Mansbridge, *Why We Lost the ERA* (Chicago: University of Chicago Press, 1986).

17 Lindsay Gibbs, "Muffet McGraw Is Done Hiring Men," *Think Progress*, March 30, 2019, https://thinkprogress.org/this-top -womens- college- basketball- coach- is-done -hiring-men-5f3b6d06609b.

18 Charlotte Carroll, "ND Coach Muffet McGraw Says 'We Don't Have Enough Women in Power,'" *Sports Illustrated*, April 4, 2019, https://www.si.com/college/2019/04 /04/muffet-mcgraw-notre-dame-coach-speaks -womens-equality.

19 Lizzy Goodman, "The Best Women's Soccer Team in the World Fights for Equal Pay," *New York Times*, June 10, 2019, https://www .nytimes.com/2019/06/10/magazine/womens -soccer-inequality-pay.html?login=google& auth=login-google.

20 Conkling, *Votes for Women*, 186–214.

21 Stacey Abrams, *Lead from the Outside: How to Build Your Future and Make Real Change* (New York: Picador, 2019).

22 Mary Beard, *Women and Power* (New York, Liverwright, 2017), 3–10.

23 Beard, *Women and Power*, 17.

24 Dobson, *Remember the Ladies*, 48–51.

25 Conkling, *Votes for Women*, 24–29.

26 Dobson, *Remember the Ladies*, 65–72.

27 Dobson, *Remember the Ladies*, 93.

28 Joan C. Williams and Sky Mihaylo, "How the Best Bosses Interrupt Bias on Their Teams," *Harvard Business Review*, November–December 2019, https://hbr.org/2019/11/how-the-best-bosses-interrupt-bias-on-their-teams.

29 Tonja Jacobi and Dylan Schweers, "Justice, Interrupted: The Effect of Gender, Ideology and Seniority at Supreme Court Oral Arguments," Northwestern University, 2017, https://papers.ssrn.com/sol3/papers.cfm?abstract_id=2933016.

30 Kathryn Heath, Jill Flynn, and Mary Davis Holt, "Women, Find Your Voice," *Harvard Business Review*, June 2014.

31 Williams and Mihaylo, "How the Best Bosses Interrupt Bias on Their Teams."

32 Beard, *Women and Power*, 13–16, 41–42.

33 Conkling, *Votes for Women*, 148–49.

34 Abigail Player, Georgina Randsley de Moura, Ana C. Leite, Dominic Abrams, and Fatima Tresh, "Overlooked Leadership Potential: The Preference for Leadership Potential in Job Candidates Who Are Men vs. Women," *Frontiers in Psychology*, April 16, 2019, https://www.frontiersin.org/articles/10.3389/fpsyg.2019.00755/full.

35 Conkling, *Votes for Women*, 225–27.

36 Conkling, *Votes for Women*, 225.

37 Mary Barmeyer O'Brien, *Jeannette Rankin: Bright Star in the Big Sky* (Lanham, MD: Two Dot Publishing, 2015).

38 Dobson, *Remember the Ladies*, 244–51.

39 Dobson, *Remember the Ladies*, 84–87.

40 Dobson, *Remember the Ladies*, 97–101.

41 Elaine Weiss, *The Woman's Hour: The Great Fight to Win the Vote* (New York: Penguin, 2019).

42 Conkling, *Votes for Women*, 39–41.

43 Susan Ware, *Why They Marched: Untold Stories of the Women Who Fought for the Right to Vote* (Cambridge, MA: Belknap Press of Harvard University Press, 2019), 29–40.